THE GREAT
AWAKENING

Volume - VI

A series of superbly informative and prophetic messages,
downloaded and transcribed originally as newsletters by

Sister Thedra

These precious messages are reprinted herein.

ISBN: 978-1-7363418-6-5

Contents

Mission Statement

Give the truth to the world. Let it be received where it will. Many will read the messages. Some will accept the truth, others will read through curiosity, a few will ridicule. Yet to all is the truth given, and to all remains the power of choice.

The hope of the world in these times is in spiritualizing all forms of activity---promoting understanding through love and service. These must be the watchwords if the world is to come into lasting peace. We are trying to influence a world that is going astray and could cause undreamed of suffering. We are trying to overcome the thought of materialists and to bring a spiritual outlook into the earthly life. We need the help of all on earth who can think in spiritual terms. The great battle to be fought now is between the spiritual and the material, between idealism and carnalism. You can help by spreading the word---we are asking that you help because the battle may be long and the victory far away.

Halls of Light is not allied with any sect, denomination, political entity, organization, neither endorses nor opposes any cause. There are no dues for membership. Halls of Light is self-supporting through its own voluntary contributions. Halls of Light has but one purpose: to help through encouragement and understanding...

To contact the publishers or to obtain copies of our other books, please contact us at email: goldtown11@gmail.com

Esu Jesus Sananda

This reproduction is from an actual photograph taken on June 1st, 1961, in Chichen Itza, Yucatan, by one of thirty archaeologists working in the area at the time. Sananda appeared in visible, tangible body and permitted His photograph to be taken.

THE SIBORS PORTIONS

Part #1

Received while crossing Lake Titicaca

Beloved -- This is MY MESSAGE unto them - that they prepare themself - that they may be brot out from the place wherein they are -- For in the time which is near - there shall be a great shock unto the Earth - which shall destroy some of Her boundaries - and this shall be a sign unto them that "the day of destruction is upon them - - So shall it profit them that they make ready themself - that they might be prepared for that which shall come upon them -- And on this I set MY SEAL - and it shall not become void -- So be it and Beleis --- Brother Bor

Beloved -- This shall be given unto the people which are yet in the places of the world - the places wherein they labor for bread - and the substance of life -- They forget wherein they are staid - and they have forgotten their inheritance - for they are lost in the valley of despair -- And they have been blinded by the forces of darkness - which FORCH upon them such conditions as they are now confronted   with -- So it is the better part of wisdom to prepare them - for the place which is prepared for then which do give ear - and prepare themself for that which shall come upon them ---

Before that shall happen - there shall be many signs - and much disturbance within the Earth- and upon Her surface - and within the air and waters -- Fire shall take its toll - and the land shall be plagued by insects and pestilence not known before -- But the people shall

1

not awaken unto the part which they have played in bringing this upon them-self -- For it is but the seeds of Satan which they have sown - and the frailties of men which set themself up - and apart from The Father - Which has sent them forth unto the Earth - which was prepared for them by The Father - and given into their keeping -- They have forgotten that the Mother Earth has nourished and healed them - and has been unto them the cradle of many lives-- And many civilizations have flourished and perished within Her arms --
-

And they forget that they have not fulfilled their covenant with Her - The Mother Earth - which received them in perfection -- For in perfection was She sent into manifestation that this age might come into fruit - and be a shining place within the firmaments -- For it is ordained by The Father - that this Earth of yours shall become a Sun unto yet uninhabited planets - which shall in turn serve them which do not awaken upon this one at present - them which We call the "Sleepers" - for they shall awaken in due season -- It is The Father's Will that they awaken - and a place is prepared for to receive them -- Not one shall be lost or overlooked - for it shall be given unto them to be put into a place wherein are many to guide and guard them - as the Guardians have guided and guarded the Earth upon Her course -- Her greatness is due unto Their guidance - for The Father gave Them charge over Her - when HE set Her upon Her appointed course - for therein is Wisdom ---

Therein is the pity - that which was created perfect has been defiled by man – Her soil depleted - Her forests ravished - Her water polluted - and Her face was pocked with great ugly scars- search of wealth - without any thot of whence cometh that which is the fortune of the Earth and Her people ---

This is their inheritance that they shall know these things -- So be it that them which do bestir themself shall become of the age of accountability - and shall receive their inheritance in full -- For the New Age brings its fulness - and them which have received their inheritance - shall remain with Then which have guarded the Earth - Then which have been Her Guardians from the beginning -- And they which shall remain shall have the keeping of the records which She holds within Her vortex -- And they shall be broken and read - and they shall be the fortune of the New Age and Her people--- For it is ordained that the Earth shall cradle a New Age - and a NEW People -- For them which shall remain as the remnant - shall be made whole - and they shall be as new ---

The Earth shall be purified - and it shall give forth a new light from the place which is appoint-ted Her within the firmaments -- There shall be a new Moon - and She shall have a New Sun - and in turn She shall be a Sun unto lesser worlds - for that is She being prepared -- Bless them which give forth the message of the New Age - for it is in preparation of the New Dawn which approaches with great speed -- And they are but Messengers of The Father -- Bless them that give of themself that these words might be recorded - and that they with ears might hear - and they with eyes which are opened might see ---

Say unto them that which ye will - but their reward cometh not from man which has tongues of asps - nor from them which are given to words of flattery-but from them which small give ear - and become one with the LIGHT which shineth bright -- And as yet it is

3

obscured by the darkness of man's own mind - which is the animal consciousness - and not The Father's - for The Father knoweth wherein man is staid - and they have forgotten! Blest is the man which has his memory - and knows from whence he came -- Before his delusions shall pass - he shall suffer much -- Then shall the GREAT DAWN come upon him which he has awaited -- For he has been asleep - and in purgatory for ages past -- Now They which have guarded move in closely - and They prepare fertile soil - to receive the seed which shall be sown in the new place ---

And They give of Themself that this might be accomplished within due season -- Blest are they which are mindful of the Guardians which are the Ones which have held the Earth steadfast -- For She is now to the age of change - and change She will! For it is the PLAN which was inaugurated on Her completion - that She shake off the old and put on the new -- And forget not that she shall flip Her axis - and therein shall be chaos - but from this shall come peace and harmony unto Her -- Much as a house cleaning She shall renew Her atoms -- She shall bring forth new flora and new fauna - for She is now finished with the old forms - and She shall take unto Herself new ones of more delicate nature ---

The birds of the air shall be iridescent and their song shall be that of another time scale - not heard by man of Earth -- They shall commune freely with man and fear him not -- They shall build nests within their hair in love and joy for their communication -- And the fauna shall serve man - and rejoice for the oneness of being - for they shall know their Father and have their memory - which man in his darkness has had blanked from him -- Be this a part of which is to come in the New Age ---

There is a glorious NEW DAWN which is now appearing unto man- which is of the NEW AGE -- And more shall be revealed unto him which seeketh after TRUTH -- For this shall he hunger - and seek - and it shall not be denied him -- First he must ask - hunger - and seek - and make ready himself - that he be worthy to receive the secrets which have been diligently hidden from the profane -- This is the better part of wisdom -- And the PLAN which so carefully was brot into manifestation ages upon ages ago is now being fulfilled --
-

And a new dispensation is given unto them which make ready themself -- Blest are they which give credence unto them of this New Dispensation -- For they are the Messengers of God The Father - Which has brot them out from the masses which remain in darkness -- Be ye not fearful - for therein is folly ---

This shall be the day of awakening - not death - for death shall be revealed as the false one - and not the reality -- For it is the 'poet' which was said that "beyond the grave is no repentance" Yet he knows not what he writes - for the grave is but the potters place of carnage - and holds not that which is REAL and Eternal ---

That which is man is not bound in flesh - and flesh cannot contain him -- For that which is flesh is but animated by that which is LIFE - and for that does he leave that which he has taken upon himself -- Before he is want to leave it (the flesh) - he experiences that which is given unto him that he might profit thereby -- And when this is accomplished/ that which he took upon himself to do - he leaves it (the flesh) and departs for yet other realms - other lessons - other experiences - that he might fulfill his destiny for which he was sent out -- Be this the LAW of the nature of manmade manifest

5

upon the Earth -- Yet as he goes on his appointed course he takes upon himself other natures of other realms - other planets and of other forms ---

This is the price he pays upon each planet and in each realm -- For this does he go out that he may experience all that is to be experienced thru physical manifestation -- Thus he gains wisdom and strength - and he once again returns unto The Father -- Fulfilled are his missions - and he has satisfied his longings - and sd he returns into The Father - he knows from whence he came - and he longs for his return -- And thus he has fulfilled his destiny -- And he may return unto physical manifestation as a great source of enlightenment - or he may work as one unembodied for the time which is - or he may choose to be a star which has not any substance other than LIGHT which is eternal - and without beginning or end - that which is known as Alpha and Omega - The force of all Creation which exists within the realm of consciousness – Beleis-

Beloved - this shall be given unto them immediately - and it shall go into that which has been begun - and for that have ye waited -- So be it that it shall be included within the BOOK OF LIGHT -- Forget not that there shall be more --- Bor

Recorded by Sister Thedra of the BROTHERHOOD OF THE

7 RAYS Lake Titicaca - Peru - Bolivia ---

A Sibor is One Illuminated of God the Father - The Cause of Being -- The Source of ALL KNOWLEDGE --

To sibor is to enlighten - to Illumine thru the Sibors - from the Realms of Light --

6

A Sibet is one which has entered the path of light - which has prepared himself to receive a Sibor --

Part #2

Blest of My being -- This is but the beginning of thy work - for it shall be given unto thee to give them the fruit - which they know not -- And they shall call it "bitter"-- And they shall choke on that which they call "sweet" -- And so be it that they shall have that which shall profit them -- And it shall be unto then succor- And they shall gather thistles wherein there is wheat -- And there shall be great sorrow within them -- And they shall be like unto the one which goes to the priest for forgiveness and finds him asleep -- And therein is the pity of it -- <u>They sleepeth at high noon</u> -- find they give naught unto the ONE which has sent them unto the Earth - and which awaits their return -- So be it that they shall awaken - and they shall have their eyes opened -- For it is come that the great and the small shall sit together - and they shall counsel with Them which have guarded them - and have held the Earth steadfast upon Her course - and they shall know wherein they are staid ---

So be it that they shall come unto the place which is prepared for them -- And they shall have that which they have portioned out for themself -- They shall have no memory of that which is now unto them real - for their illusions shall pass as the shadows before the noon day Sun -- And they shall have the same fortune which their illusions have created - and it shall be unto them a prison wall. ---

For until every vestige of their illusions and wanton is removed from them - they shall be in bondage -- An with My own hands I shall be unto them bondsman -- I shall give unto then of Myself - My Heritage - My Grace - and I shall stand ready to deliver them out of their own self-created hell - when they seek Me -- For I AM the LIGHT and the WAY - and I have given of Myself that they might now Me - and that they might find their way unto The Father - which has sent then forth -- So shall they come of their own "free will" - for it is the way which was given unto them ---

And it shall profit them to find their own way -- And they shall be within their own right to call themself Sons of God -- And they shall receive their Inheritance and become equal unto HIM ---

And it is fortuned unto some to come at the call of the Clarions -- Some shall wait for the Condors - and some shall wait until the last trumpet is sounded -- And others shall go into their new place in deep sleep - and they shall be rendered service - according to their ability to receive and to comprehend -- And these which are asleep shall find their sleep disturbed and restless - and these which are awake shall be watchful and alert - and their LIGHT shall be expanded - and it shall burn upon the altar wherein I AM -- And there shall be great power within their LIGHT - and they shall be known by that LIGHT - and they shall be sought out - and they shall be found -- And so be it that the NEW DAY DAWNETH - and they shall find themself within another world - which they have fortuned unto themself ---

And give unto them this Portion - for it is the better part of wisdom that they be given that which is for them ---

And that which is for thyself keep for thyself therein is wisdom -- And so be it that they shall call out -- And they which hunger shall be fed and shall find Me -- And I shall be glad to receive them wherein I AM -- And there shall be great joy -

And then which turn their face from Me - shall be unable to receive MY WORDS nor My Prophets -- for they find no PEACE - and they shall cry Lord! and shall look within the closets - for that which they shall have within their mouths hollow words fortune them self these frivolous prayers - which words - that avail them naught -- And so shall it not profit them ---

Blest are they which cry out - for they shall be heard -- Blest are they which give ear for they shall hear -- Blest are they which come into the Place wherein I AM - or they shall return unto darkness no more - and they shall overcome all things -- And they shall have dominion over Heaven and Earth - for they shall receive their inheritance - and they shall be equal with God - and for that have they waited -- So be it their waiting shall end -- And so be it that many are called - and few are chosen -- And them which are chosen are the ones which have prepared themself that they might be My LAMP BEARERS -- And they shall walk wherein I shall lead them - and they shall be unto themself true -- And they shall know no sorrow- and darkness shall not ensnare them - and they shall receive that which has been kept for them -- And it shall be the Father's good pleasure to receive them home unto HIMSELF ---

That which has been loosed within the Earth for eons of time - which has bound them - and which has taken unto itself the form of the black dragon - shall be removed from the Earth - and shall be expressed upon the Earth no more ---

There is but the ETERNAL form - and that is the beginning and the end - and that which has no beginning and no end - and it is soundless - and yet is all sound - and within it is contained all that

10

IS -- And therein is The Eloheim - and the "ALL" Which has <u>never ceased to BE</u> - and which ever remains the same ---

And for them which shall remain true unto the Source - shall be given dominion over all that which has been bound within the Earth and within the places of darkness ---

<u>And so shall they which remain steadfast- and true to their Source be ascended</u> - and they shall see and know all things -- And the LAW of the Earth shall not bind them - and the attraction of the Moon shall not be unto them a poison -- Blest are they which are free from the gravitation of the Earth - and the attraction of the Moon - for they shall have dominion over the Earth and all things therein -- And therein they are free to go unto other planets within the galaxy from which they come - and such is dominion in The Father's House ---

And there shall be a great awakening - and a great gathering in - and there shall be much joy and gladness -- And so be it and beleis ---

Blessings unto all which receive MY <u>loving offering -- And them which receive MY WORDS unto themself - I shall reward with much understanding and wisdom - and it shall suffice them -- And so be it and Beleis</u> - Sananda

Recorded by Sister Thedra of the Brotherhood of The 7 Rays --

- Lake Titicaca - Peru - Bolivia ---

Part #3

Sara : -- Beloved Ones of Earth - has it not been long since ye went from Me in all your pristine purity? And now it is given unto Me to open the way for thy return - and so shall ye return in due time -- And ye shall be made to KNOW that which is TRUTH - and that which is the Ordinance of The Father -- And ye shall stand forth - a testimony of that which thy Elder Brother has said -- And ye shall be risen from the dead - and ye shall know death no more -- And it shall be that the grave shall be as a tomb no longer -- For it shall be given unto every man to KNOW that which The Master Sananda knew when He resurrected Himself - and stept forth in His Holy Christ Body - which is indestructible - everlasting - knowing no pain or suffering ---

So shall it be unto every man - for that has the veil of Maya been parted -- And it shall behoove every man to look unto The Father - The Source of his Being for his sustenance -- For the Earth shall provide only misery and woe for him who knows not The Father -- And they which seek The Father - all things shall be added in <u>love and harmony</u> -- And PEACE shall abide within him - and he shall be brot into the Place wherein <u>all</u> things are known - and wherein is LOVE and WISDOM only -- And they shall have that which has been kept for them - and that which is their inheritance ---

So shall they have their place within the Eternal Place which is provided for them -- And they shall know The Father – from Which they have gone out - and they shall return into darkness no more -- For this has the dispensation been given unto ye children of Earth -

- And WE Which are of the Etheric Realm reach out to thee - that ye might be lifted up ---

And so shall ye know US - and the part WE have with thee -- For it is long since ye have been in darkness -- And may ye stir thyself - and be ye quickened unto The LIGHT which WE shed upon thee - that ye might find the way back home ---

And wherein ye shall have the whole ARMOR OF GOD The Father given unto thee - and ye shall be as a wayfarer of Satan no more -- So shall ye be brot to the age of accountability - thru the New Dispensation -- And ye shall be given the Precepts and the Portions of The Father's Work - which ye are capable of comprehending -- So shall ye do according to thy own free will -- Yet it shall profit thee to say: "Father - Thy WILL be done in me - and thru me - and by me - and for me" ---

And in this manner shall it be given unto thee to find thy way home - and therein is much wisdom -. And it shall profit thee to ponder this - for it shall profit thee much! And as I abide with The Father - and He has invested within Me the authority to be unto thee Sibor - I shall give unto thee that which has been withheld - lo these eons of time -- and ye shall be as one awakened from the dead -- For it is given unto Those which abide with The Father to know all things - and to comprehend the LAW which governs Them -- And it is given unto Them to give succor unto the Earth and Her Children - and they shall be brot unto the Place from which they went out---

Give unto Them thy love and thy thanks - for it is Their only reward - that ye perceive of Their Teaching - and give ear and obedience unto Their call -- And Their reward shall be great indeed

- for many shall hear and heed the call -- And forget not that there shall be a great awakening - and a great gathering in -- And it shall be given unto this generation to see the Ones which are of the Etherial Worlds and to communicate with Them -- And they shall no longer be called crazy! And for that matter the age of martyrdom is past -- For no longer shall the workers in the LIGHT of THE CHRIST be brot before Pilate -- And they shall have their legirons cut away -- And forget not that they which cry; "imposter - fools - or crazy"- shall be brot to account for their foolishness - before the Throne of Justice -- And they shall be bound by their own injustice -- And so be it and Beleis ---

Now heed ye this - for it is said: "There is none so foolish as them which think themself wise" -- And so it is! For the wise are prudent - and silent - when it is wise to keep silent -- And they speak with wisdom and prudence - which are sent unto thee - as Sibors -- For foolish talk is not part of Them -- And ye shall take heed of the speech - for it is given unto the children of darkness to say that which is prompted by darkness -- And they are not inspired by The LIGHT of The Father -- And the Eternal Verities shall be revealed unto them which seek -- So be it and Selah ---

Before thy bondage of darkness shall be lifted - ye shall give thyself whole heartedly unto the LIGHT which never fails - and it shall be unto thee all knowledge -- And all that is required of thee is to surrender up unto The Father - Son and Holy Ghost - thy own "free will"- and to walk in "His Will" -- And this shall be of thy own free will! - for it is given unto thee - as ye would have it and ye shall find thy own way -- For no man shall bring thee against thy will - and ye shall tarry in darkness as long as ye will - or ye shall arise and come into thy Father's House which is prepared for thee! - and therein is wisdom -- Now is the day of thy deliverance from the chains which has bound thee in the world of men - and wherein is darkness and sorrow -- I ask of thee only one thing - to seek - and ye shall be rewarded ---

For there is the LAW which shall be fulfilled -- And no one escapes the LAW which the child of Earth must come to know and obey-- Blest is the seeker after the LIGIT which is Eternal - and shineth within the Place wherein are they which are rescued from darkness - and from bondage ---

So shall man come to walk and counsel with the Ones of the LIGHT which are eternally with The Father - for therein is the Will of God The Father -- And so be it -- And blest are they which are the Messengers of The Father for they shall be listed up - and they shall sit on the right hand of God! And they shall know wherein they are staid ---

Be ye prepared for that which shall come upon the Earth - and that which shall come upon thee -- For it is given unto the Earth to be reborn - and unto thee to have a NEW PLACE of abode - and therein is much wisdom -- For the Earth shall have a resting period- and ye shall be put into a NEW PLACE which has been prepared for thee -- And it shall provide thee as a schoolroom of a Higher Order - and there shall be Sibors of the Highest Order for the world of men-- And they shall learn the LAW which has not been revealed unto them in the past ages ---

This is the "New Age" and a "New Order" and a New Dispensation is given unto thee - which shall be thy salvation -- And so be it that ye shall respond unto the call which shall go out into all the nations of the Earth -- And it shall echo thru all the lands of the Earth! And ye shall be unto thyself true - and ye shall listen unto them which shall call unto thee -- And they shall see thee in all places of the Earth - and there is no hiding place -- And so shall ye be within the law to claim the "Sonship" with The Father - and to give unto HIM credit for thy being -- And ye shall give unto HIM the glory - and the praise -- And ye shall falter not - nor shall ye stumble -- Blest are they which lift up their eyes unto The Father - for they shall be opened - and they shall see - and know that which they see -- And so be it and Selah ---

Give unto US thy hands and thy heart - and ye shall be led into places which are prepared for thee - and which have been kept for thee -- And ye shall know hunger and longing no more - and for that have ye frofited ---

Before ye shall enter into the Temple of The Living God - ye shall be made clean - and for that has many been sent unto thee -- And it is thy inheritance to be cleansed and renewed - for it is given unto every man to have the pore renewed -- And this is the PLAN which Jesus/ Sananda - The Son of God - demonstrated unto the people which failed to hear the Message -- And now it is given unto thee again -- And ye shall stand forth within thy glorified bodies made new! And for that has He come unto them which have sought Him out -- Forget not that He walks in the garment of flesh in the world of men -- And as they comprehend Him not - and they know Him not - and as they seek Him - comprehension is given unto them -- And it shall be given unto many to sup with Him and to counsel with Him - and therein is wisdom ---

And they shall have their heads unbound - and the veil of Maya shall be removed - and there shall be great joy - and much gladness! And for the first time I say unto thee - be ye prepared - for I shall walk among thee - and I shall bring thee a PLAN which shall be unto thee new - and unto thee PEACE and LIGHT - and ye shall see it and follow it - and ye shall know freedom as ye have not known it -- And so be it and Selah ---

Be ye alert and have thy affairs in order - for there shall be a loud Voice call from afar - and it shall be given unto thee to hear it - and ye shall respond in haste! And be ye quickened that ye might know the Voice and follow it - it shall profit thee -- And ye shall be as one poured out - for it shall be in no wise given unto thee to go astray -- And ye shall know the day of deliverance has come and ye shall be glad! And this is the beginning of thy fortune - for it shall be given unto thee to have upon thy forehead a star - and that shall signify ye are reborn -- And ye shall be within the LAW to call thyself God - and this shall be thy Inheritance - given unto thee by The Father - and therein is wisdom and mastery over all things -- And so shall ye awaken unto thy own LIGHT - which is Eternal and which is The Christ -- And ye shall be free forever from the bondage of darkness ---

And as this Portion which is given unto thee goes out - it is given unto them which are My hands made manifest - to have within them the power to go into the Secret Places which have been hidden from the imprudent and the unjust - and which shall be opened up unto them which are prepared - and them which have proven themself worthy of the trust which shall be invested within them -- And again I say - give unto The Father thy while self - thy hands - thy heart -

thy will - and it shall avail thee much good -- And ye shall know such joy as ye have never known -- Now is the time for much action and ther shall be much going and coming -- And there shall be an exchange between the children of Earth and other planets -- Some of the Earth shall have Initiations on other planets - and return as Messengers of them which have sibored them -- And glad shall ye be that ye have known these things - for they shall be unto thee a SHIELD and BUCKLER -- And ye shall be sufficient unto thyself - and therein is wisdom ---

Before thee is the gate - and ye have the power to open it - and the path is strait - and ye cannot error upon it - for there is but one direct course which leads home -- And for that have WE come that ye might enter the PATH which is bright and strait ---

And WE stand guard and ready to answer thy call by day or by night -- And ye shall be sustained in thy search for the gate - and it shall open wide before thee -- It is a plain and powerful part which shall forewarn thee - and give thee courage and strength -- And it shall carry within these WORDS - Our never failing LOVE and LIGHT-- For long have We watched in silence - and held thee within Our Bosom -- And long have We waited to bring thee home -- And the age of speech has come - when the doors shall open wide unto US - and so shell We speak - with much gladness and authority -- And ye shall know Us - as We know each other - for We shall come unto thee and ye shall counsel with Us as fellow Beings - and therein is the New Age -- For We shall serve thee as Friend - and Counsellor - and as Older Brothers and Sisters -- In no wise shall We intrude - but when ye call - We shall respond within WISDOM and LOVE - at any time and any place ---

I All prepared to be Hostess unto them - who are prepared to come into My Place of Abode - and I shall be glad to receive them - - And ye shall be glad to be within My place - and there shall be many to receive thee -- And there shall be a great gathering together - and the music shall peal out thru the Cosmos - and it shall be heard - and it shall bless them which have ears that hear -- And such is a part of thy fortune which has been kept for thee -- And so be it given unto thee when ye have become to the age of accountability -- And this is the WILL of The Father - that ye all graduate from the School of Earth - and enter into the Eternal Verities - and the PLAN shall be revealed unto thee -- And I stand ready to be unto thee hands and feet -- Ye have but to reach out and I All with thee and at thy service in the Name of The Father - Son and Holy Ghost - Amen---

Blessings from the Throne of The Father - and the Fortune or the Mother - which holds thee near and dear -- I AM thy Mother Saraof The Order of The Emerald Cross ---

Recorded by Sister Thedra of The Emerald Cross

Part #4

Beloved Ones - which are My sheep - and which have been given unto My care by The Father - and by The Mother Sara – I AM within the Earth - and upon the Earth made manifest -- I Walk in a garment of flesh - even as ye -- And I go and come within the places wherein ye are -- And I give of Myself that ye might know Me - and yet ye have not sought lie - and ye comprehend Me not -- Yet the time is at hand that ye shall call out - and ye shall be in the straits of darkness - and ye shall not know the joy which is allotted unto them which seek the LIGHT early -- For they which seek the LIGHT early - shall be lifted up - and they shall escape the sorrow and suffering which shall come upon the Earth ---

For the time of disaster is near at hand - and there shall be great suffering - and it is given unto lie to bring unto thee LIGHT and PEACE -- And within the time which is allotted unto Me - I shall do My utmost to awaken thee from thy lethargy - and I shall give all that ye can assimilate - and more! So be ye as one which has ears - and listen unto what I say unto thee - for it shall profit thee much! I AM now within the secret place of My abode - and I AM in the place prepared to receive them which seek Me out - for it is the LAW that ye seek to find Me ---

And as ye seek My Presence - so shall I come unto thee - and I shall give of Myself that ye might comprehend that which shall be given unto thee of The Father - and The Mother -- So shall ye be prepared for thy new place of abode -- For it is prepared for thee - and it shall provide thee the place wherein ye may learn the NEW LAW - which has been revealed unto them which has been brot out of the darkness - and that which is now to be revealed unto the men of Earth ---

These are the "Divine Ordinances" of The Father - and the Precepts which have been held in trust for man - until this age which has now come - and for this dispensation -- So be it that they shall be quickened - and they shall be as ones which have ears that hear - and eyes that see -- So shall they walk with the Ones which are sent to sibor them -- And there are many sent of The Father - even as I AM sent -- And there shall be many more sent - for there shall be a great army of workers within the LIGHT -- which shall descend upon the Earth that She might be brot out of darkness - and prepared for Her new part -- For it is given unto Earth to become a Sun unto the place wherein some of the Earthlings shall be put -- For it is given unto some to be put into a place which is new - and which has been created new for this PLAN which is now unfolding unto thee - - And the Earth shall serve as a Sun unto it ---

And for the first time it is told thee - that the Directors of this Solar System have worked for a long time to bring the Earth into her new berth - that She might come into Her heritage for which She was created in the beginning -- Now it shall be given unto the men of the Earth to become gods and to become one with The Father - and to receive their inheritance for which they have waited -- And now it is time that ye awaken and stand within the LIGHT which is shed upon the Earth at this time ---

And be ye alert - for there shall be a great Voice ring out unto the people - and they which are alert shall hear - and they which have their fingers in their ears shall not hear -- So be it that I shall give of Myself that ye may hear - and ye shall be given a hearing

21

when ye call out -- For I stand ready to answer thee - and to understand thy fortune of darkness -- And as ye fortune thyself My offer of help - so shell it be given unto thee---

And now ye shall be in the places wherein ye are prepared for that which shall be given unto thee - for there shall be many which are sent unto thee by The Father - to be Sibor unto thee -- And He has given of Himself that they might come unto thee - and that ye shall be prepared for the New Age -- And it shall behoove every man to make ready himself - that he may stand in the Presence of God The Father - for this is the day of Salvation - and ye shall profit therein -- And now it is given unto Me to be even as ye - in the places of the Earth wherein are children os many planets - which have come into the Earth at this time - to usher in the New Age - and to fulfill the LAW -- And to fulfill the Scriptures which is written within the stones of the Earth - and upon parchment - which have been protected from the unscrupulous and the infamous -- And so shall they be brot out for man's edification in the Age which is to come---

Many shall sit and counsel with Me in My secret abode - and read the ancient records - which are in no wise the figment of any scholars imagination - and they shall speak for themself -- And they who have fortuned unto themself that privilege - shall go into the places of the Earth as My Messengers -- And they shall be received as My authority -- And they shall be as My Lamp Bearers -- And they shall give of themself - even as I give unto them ---

And ye shall receive in the Name of The Father - Son and Holy Ghost - and so be it that it shall profit thee -- And within the time which is near - One shall go out from My place of abode - and he shall give unto thee many things which shall seem strange - and new unto thee - and yet it is <u>eternally the same</u> - for it is now revealed unto thee - that which has been hidden from thee -- And now it is given unto them which seek TRUTH to be given these things - which shall be unto them their SHIELD and BUCKLER within the days ahead -- For now I say unto thee - <u>unless ye ask</u> - it shall remain hidden - and therein is wisdom -- Ye give not the flesh of the animal unto babes at the breast - for it is the LAW that when ye are ready ye ask - and The Father stands ready to supply thy needs ---

And it is such that not one shall be forgotten - or overlooked -- For there are many within thy midst which can pluck thee out at any moment - and give thee that which is necessary unto thee-- And so shall ye look within thine own self for the LIGHT - that ye may be alert unto thy Brother's LIGHT - for LIGHT is like unto Itself - It attracts more LIGHT -- And for that have I made Myself manifest unto them which have sought Me --

And as they have sought Me - their LIGHT has expanded - and It has been added unto Mine - that the whole Earth might become a Sun -- And therein is <u>great</u> <u>revelation</u> unto thee ---

For as the man of Earth is lifted up - so is the Earth - that She might fulfill Her Mission -- And be ye fruitful unto The Father - for He has given thee <u>permission</u> - to be within the Earth for the fulfilling of this age ---

And that is a privilege given unto thee of God The Father -- And it is given unto Me to speak unto thee - as I have not for the past years of the "Silent period" -- And the silence shall be broken in all the lands of the Earth - and again I shall walk the byways and the hiways - and be as ye -- And as ye come into the age of comprehension - I shall sit and counsel thee - and I shall teach thee the PRECEPTS of The Father - which has sent Me unto thee - that ye might awaken unto thy own "Sonship" and be as the wayfarer of Satan no more ---

And it is indeed wise to ask of The Father - that ye might receive Me - for in no wise shall I intrude upon thy free will -- And yet it is the WILL of The Father that I bring thee out of darkness -- And for that do I wait - that ye may come as ye are called - and by thy own free will -- And this is for the ones which have as yet not learned the wisdom of saying: "Father - Thy WILL be done in me - thru me - by me - and for me" ---

And therein is the KEY unto thy legirons - which have bound thee -- And be ye as one which knows wherein ye are bound - and wherein is thy freedom ---

I shall be unto thee bondsman - and I stand ready to loose thee of thy bondage at thy request -- And ye have but to seek the LIGHT which is of The Father -- And ye shall be unerring in thy search - and not falter -- And ye shall be unto thyself true - and ye shall have no other masters before God The Father -- For as ye seek thy own salvation within HIM - many shall be sent to deliver thee up -- And this is the PLAN which has been prepared for thy salvation ---

And the time is at hand when all shall be removed from the Earth for a period - for She shall be made new - and She shall rest -- For in no wise has She been in the place clean - and She has been defiled - and herein is the pity of Her plight -- For every atom of the Earth shall be cleansed and made new - even as ye children of the Earth -

- And ye too shall be cleansed and given new bodies - without the throes of rebirth - and that is as it shall be - for it is given unto me to know - and to comprehend the LAW which governs these things of which I speak -- Now ye shall rest assured I AM in the Earth for a PLAN which shall be fulfilled! And not a PLAN goes astray -- I shall be unto thee Sibor - and I shall deliver thee out of darkness at thy speaking - and ye have only to speak the word - and I AM at thy service - in the Name of The Father - Mother Sara and The Holy Ghost - Amen ---

Be ye blest of My Being - and of them within the secret places which stand ready to serve thee -- And may ye be as one quickened - that ye may comprehend that which has been given unto thee -- I AM thy Elder Brother - and faithful servant in the LIGHT of The Christ - which I represent and hold out unto thee --- Sananda -- Order of The Emerald Cross ----

Recorded by Sister Thedra of the Emerald Cross

Part #5

Blest of My Being: As ye begin this day it shall be given unto thee to have that which is prepared for thee and it shall be given unto thee by thy Brother Bor -- And it shall be for them which await the Words of the Sibors Who are waiting to speak - and ye shall be unto them His hand and His mouth - and so be ye prepared for that which shall be given unto thee this day -- It shall be for the good of All -- And blest are they which are the Messengers of the Father - for they shall be lifted up and they shall sit on the right hand of God - the

Father

Beloved - thy Brother Bor speaketh - And now I shall say that which I have waited to say unto thee -- And be ye as one which has a mind to comprehend - for it is My part to give unto thee that which ye of Earth know little about - and that is "ethics! -- The ethics of which I speak is but the better part of wisdom -- For it is in the place wherein I am that all the plans for thy freedom - which is founded upon ethics was planned ---

It had its beginning within My place of abode - and it shall have its ending within this place -- For in the days and years ahead shall ye come to know the meaning of the word "ethic" ---

And so be it that not a person which has set himself up as an authority has the full knowledge of its meaning -- Now in the New Age it shall be revealed unto thee in all its better and higher aspects -- Now within the time which is near at hand - there shall be much sorrow and want -- And I have come unto thee from the place wherein all things are made known -- And I shall endeavor to give

26

thee a portion of that which I have seen and which has already come to pass within the place wherein We are ---

There is much that has been done within the laboratories of the scientists - and behind locked doors and drawn curtains -- And it has been done in the name of "progress" -- And now will ye permit Me to present My side for just a moment -- For now it is come that many shall suffer from the illness which has been brought about thru the laboratory tests which are daily being made and which is done without regard to the Plan of the Father which has created ALL within the kingdom of man perfect -- And they who give themself up to the experiments of the scientists are but tools in the hands of satanic forces -- Now when it is apparent that there be an illness which is in no wise given unto them to heal - they put to bear a pressure which gives the patient a part which could be spared him - - and which becomes a mental torture which he carries into his next body as leg irons -- And it is sometimes revealed unto him within his tortured sleep - or it takes the form of great fears whithin his wakeful hours - Which in turn - brings on another disease ---

Now My beloved ones - wherein has man profited by his science - when he fails to release the man who stands revealed in his true light? Be ye alert and hear Me in this - for it shall be given again and again -- And ye shall have the stigma removed ---

Be ye want to hear - then pay ye shall - for it is given unto Me to say this: that the black dragon of the dark forces shall be slain -- And he shall hold forth in the world of men no longer -- And it shall be given unto Me to go into the places of darkness and bring them out - and to expose them to the Light -- And to give unto the children of the Earth - Light - which is the weapon that shall slay the black dragon --

Now My children - who have begun to stir in thy sleep - listen and ye shall learn many things which ye have not hitherto been told —

For in no wise am I here to play a foolish game - or a loose one -- Ye shall be within thy places prepared for that which shall become common bond unto thee - that is suffering - and it makes all men brothers -- Be as ones which can comprehend these things - for it shall be unto thee thy salvation ---

And in no wise are We Who come to thee in the mood for entertaining thee -- And now be it such that the alarm has gone out! And the cry shall be heard within the time which is near -- And many shall stand ready to release them which have given of themselves - and which are prepared -- And the cry! Oh- the cry - which sounds within the night - how sad - how sad! ---

So be ye as one which has given unto the Father - of thy time and of thy self -- And there shall be a great gathering up -- And ye shall be within thy beds and yet ye shall be brot out -- And ye shall be given that which has been kept for thee ---

Blest shell ye be which give Me audience - for I shall walk in thy midst and I shall put upon thy forehead a mark - and ye shall be known unto them in the days of disaster -- When it is come that the Voice is heard - ye shall give thyself up wholly unto it and follow it - for it shall be unto thee try deliverance - For it is the Plan of the Father that ye be rescued within the time of holocaust -- And it is given unto Me to prepare thee that there may be order - and less panic that I reveal these things unto thee -- Be ye as one which has been drilled for a fire - or an accident at sea - and profit by the words I give unto thee - for in the time which is near ye shall remember them ---

Wherein is it recorded that there shall be "winds" and that the Earth shall shift upon her axis? And so be it that there shall be a great shock which shall rock her foundations -- Yet that should be of no concern unto thee - for the places are provided for thee -- And ye shall be concerned only with thy preparation - which shall profit thee -- And glad ye shall be that ye have prepared thy self -- For in that time ye shall stand revealed in thy true light and ye shall be known as ye are -- For it is given unto Them Who shall come as thy rescuers to know thee in truth and in Reality with thy mask of Earth removed -- Be ye as one which can step forth in the Light of the Christ made Whole -- And ye shall not be afraid and nothing can prevail against thee -- As the time draws nigh the flood gates shall open and great Light shall be given unto them which have eyes that see -- And as the Mother of Us has said unto thee "be ye quickened that ye may be receptive to the Light We shed upon thee" ---

For We give of Our Love -- Our efforts are given for the purpose of bringing thee safely home -- And as ye read these words make them thy own - for thee solely have I given them -- And while ye ponder them ye shall be quickened - and ye shall be given the mind to comprehend -- Be ye as one which gives of his love and his energy unto the Light -- And when it is come that ye shall stand face to face with thy self - ye shall be glad that ye have been given that which has prepared thee ---

Which shall profit thee more - to be as ye are within thy slumber - or to awaken and inherit the Kingdom of thy Father? And give unto Him credit for thy Being - and He shall be unto thee ALL that ye need -- And He has given unto thee thy Holy Estate and to Him ye shall return - And be ye as one which has gone out and as one which has returned -- And ye shall be glad thy deliverance has come ---

Go into the 'Secret Place' and give unto the Father thy self - entrust to Him thy Being - and give Him credit for thy Being -- And ye shall be in the bosom of Him which has sent thee out --

Now when ye have gathered unto thyself - then which ye shall call thy own - give unto them that which I have given unto thee -- And prepare them in the Way I have endeavored to prepare thee--

And I shall be unto thee Comforter -- I shall give unto thee My promise that ye shall be comforted ---

And blest are they which prepare the little ones - for they shall not be responsible for that which they say or do -- Yet the parents shall be held accountable - and for that has many come unto thee that ye be prepared -- They give thee instructions while ye sleep - and give thee signs - indications of that which shall be -- And They which are Messengers of the Father have given thee warning and ye have forgotten so soon! Be ye a mind to remember and hear -- Will it not profit thee? Be ye glad that the time is come for it is the Glad Age when man shall know freedom! ---

And he shall stand upon the precepts of the Divine Director which has prepared thee for this day -- And so be it such as man has no known in ages past - for he shall come and go within the galaxy as Gods -- And they shall create unto the Glory of the Father - and therein is Godhood and mastery over all things ---

Blest are they which prepare themself for their Godhood -- It is said that the Earth is a school room for Gods - so it is -- And be ye as one which has upon thy head a crown - and walk which way it tilts not -- Blest are they which give of themself that others may be prepared -- And they shall be lifted up -- Now receive My blessings and My service -- For I shall come unto thee with greater messages and much wisdom - for it is given unto Me to give unto thee as ye can comprehend -- And as ye ask - more shall be revealed unto thee --

I Am thy Elder Brother Bor -- Brotherhood of the Emerald Cross ---

Recorded by Sister Thedra of the Emerald Cross

Part #6

Beloved or My Being - Now ye shall arise and make ready thy self for the part which I shall give unto them - and it shall profit them -- And so be it and Beleis ---

Beloved of My Being - there are none within My place which are not My equal - and have They not received Their Sonship of the Father - which has given Us each Our inheritance? ---

And for that have We reached out unto thee that ye too may receive thine -- And that ye might have that which has been kept for thee -- Be ye as one which has upon thy head a crown - and walk which way it tilts not -- For it is given unto thee to be the "Children of Light" ---

And ye have been within the places of darkness so long ye have forgotten thy identity -- Now many shall come unto thee that ye might remember - and that ye night walk within the Light of the Christ -- Wherein ALL things are known and remembered -- And wherein all things are possible ---

So shall it be the Will of the Father that ye shall have a new place of abode - and ye shall be prepared for it -- For that has many been sent unto Earth - which walk among thee - and which give unto thee of their love and wisdom in discretion - and they have been unto their trust true -- They have given only that which is given unto them of the Father - that which shall profit thee - They have not asked for themself aught -- And they have gone the long way to give unto thee that which shall bring thee out of thy stupor -- For surely ye have not been alert! And ye shall become alert!

For it is given unto many to see that the whole of the worlds population stirs themselves - and therein is wisdom -- For in the time which is near We shall make known Ourself unto every one which has one iota of comprehension -- For it is come that the day of deliverance is at hand - and ye shall have the veil of maya removed forever ---

Now is the time to give thanks unto the Father for thy Being -- For in ages past ye have traveled the path in darkness and ye have been blinded to thy own Light -- And now ye shall stand forth as one illuminated - the child of God the Father -- Ye shall go into the places which have been prepared for thee in dignity and honor -- Ye shall be unto him the Glory - and ye shall be unto him the gladness of His Heart ---

And be ye prepared -- for the day of thy salvation is at hand -- and ye shall be lifted up as the condor lifts the lamb -- Ye shall be put into thy new place wherein ye shall be received with love and understanding ---

Now it is given unto Me by thy Shepherd - and every shepherd knows his sheep -- It is given unto the shepherd to gather then in and feed them -- I am in the place wherein ye shall be gathered in -- It is prepared for thee - and there are many which shall be therein to receive thee -- There shall be great joy and much gladness!---

And will ye not hear My Voice and will ye not hear My words which I say unto thee? - I am within the Earth - with a garment of flesh -- I am free (in the service of My Father which has given Me My Inheritance) to go and come -- Free from the Earth's gravitation and the attraction of the moon ---

And it is given unto many which have gone the "Royal Road" to be within the place wherein I am and to communicate freely with the Father - and to go and come at His bidding ---

Now ye shall be prepared for thy new dispensation -- for it is a New Age - a New Order and a New Dispensation is given that ye may become of age -- That thy inheritance shall be given unto thee - and ye shall profit thereby ---

Now is the day in which ye shall know the "Truth" and it shall unbind thee -- And ye shall stand forth a "Child of Light" and ye shall Know thy Father - and ye shall have no other gods before Him.

Yet as thou seeketh the Father - thy Source - many of His POINTERS shall point the way unto Him -- And ye shall know them and follow them - for it is given unto them to know the Royal Road and it is Their lot to bring thee safely home ----

Blest are the Pointers for they have prepared Themself that They might be unto thee Light - that ye may find thy way and stumble not upon the way -- Now be ye mindful of thy help and from whence it cometh - for therein is wisdom -- And ye shall become aware of the help and wherein ye are staid -- For in the time which is near there shall be reason to seek help - and it shall behoove thee to be forearmed -- And to be fore warned is to be forearmed--

And many stand ready to reach out unto thee that ye may walk with surety and steadiness ---

Before the day of thy discomfort ye shall look into the Father for thy deliverance -- And ye shall give Him of thy self and ye shall bring them within thy charge unto the Altar -- Ye shall give unto them that which ye have received - and ye shall be unto them sibor - even as I am unto thee -- For it is given unto Me of the Father that I give unto thee - and ye shall give unto them ---

Forget not that there shall be much sorrow and such suffering -- Yet it is within thy power to be in thy place delivered --

And ye shall not be as ones 'left' and as the ones which have been unto themself traitor -- For therein is the pity - when one betrays himself - the pity - the pity! For he has given unto himself the husks from the belly of the swine -- When the Father calls him home - he has his fingers in his ears and he hears nothing save the rumbling of his stomach ---

Be ye as one which has ears that hear and eyes that see -- And I am with thee and I shall touch thee that thy blindness might be healed - and that thy ears might be opened -- Give Me that which is Mine and I shall give unto thee that which is thine -- Ye shall go into thy secret chambers and seek Me out - and I shall come unto thee and I shall counsel thee -- Be ye as one which can comprehend that which I say unto thee -- I have given thee a part of that which I have for thee - and as ye ask and seek - more shall be revealed -- For the day of great revelation is here -- and My arm is not shortened -- For I am at My Father's business and He has made all things possible -- So be ye alert and ye shall learn many things which have been covered and which shall be uncovered -- And ye shall be in the place wherein ye are prepared - that ye might know and comprehend ---

Blest are they which seek the Father and there are many to sustain thee in thy search -- And blest are they which are the

Messengers of the Father -- for they shall be lifted up and they shell sit on the right hand of God the Father --

And it is My part to give unto thee of myself and of My services -- It is My part to come unto thee in the world of men made flesh- and I shall know thee -- And as ye seek Me out I shall give unto thee comprehension that ye may recognize Me -- And there shall be much gladness - - -

I shall give unto thee that which ye have hungered for - and that which ye have sought - the Peace that surpasseth all understanding ---

Be ye blest of My Being - and so be it unto thee in the Name of the Father - Son and Holy Ghost - and the Blessed Mother or Us, Sara -

I AM your Elder Brother and Servant in the Light of Christ -
Amen – Sananda

Recorded by Sister Thedra of The Brotherhood of the 7 Rays –

Lake Titicaca - Peru - Bolivia –

Part #7

Blest of My Being – Now ye shall give unto them which await My words this portion – Ye shall give unto them that which has been withheld – Has it not been said that thy hands shall be untied? And so be it that ye shall have thy head unbound and ye shall stand within the place wherein I am – Ye shall now as I know and ye shall be the hands of Sara made manifest – So be it and Beleis ---

Be ye as ones which stand within the Light which I give unto thee – For I am in the world of men that ye may be as one which stands within the Holy Christ Light – and that ye may be made Whole ---

Now ye are to be alert and listen for a Voice which shall ring out – Ye shall be made to hear and it shall profit thee – Be in the place wherein ye are prepared for that which ye shall be given – For there is much in store for thee – Within the time which is near ye shall receive that which has been kept for thee – for this time – Ye shall be given according to thy comprehension – But in no wise shall it be forced upon thee – Ye shall be of a mind to accept that which shall be given – For that is the law – For it is given unto Me to know that which is lawful and ethical ---

Ye shall be as one which has "thy own free will" and no one shall trespass upon thy privilege – and it is a privilege given unto thee by the Father – to have the Sibors which are sent by Him to sibor thee – Ye shall give unto them ear and ye shall give them thy attention and respect – For they are Ambassadors of the Father which has opened the door that ye may pass – Ye shall pass the Porter and the Pounder which are the keepers of the Gate ---

And in the time which is near ye shall enter the Inner Temple wherein is the Divine Director and the One which has given thee permission to pass ---

Go into thy secret place and give unto Him thanks that ye have the privilege of being within the Earth at this time --- For blest are they which are privileged to enter the activities of this great age – It is indeed an age where man and angel shall wall together as brothers ---

For in tine which is at hand many shall go into the places which are prepared – and they shall return as Ambassadors or Emissaries of their Sibors – They shall be as one which has been inbound – And they shall speak with Divine Authority – for they shall know – and know that they Know ---

Now ye shall choose thy own way – but I am with thee that ye may choose the open way that leads to the Father – the Source of thy Being – Ye shall be in no wise as the foolish virgins for ye shall have oil – and I shall be unto thee Light ---

Be ye as one which has gone out and as one which has returned – I am the one which has stood guard at the gate that none other shall pass that is not prepared – And ye shall be in the port made ready for embarkation – For in the time which is near thy name shall be called and ye shall respond – And ye shall know the day of thy deliverance is come ---

I am not of a mind to let thee forget – for I am sent that ye may be up and about thy salvation – and ye shall heed My words – and be as one who knows wherein ye are staid --- Believe upon thy

Father and give thyself into His keeping – and ye shall be rewarded three-fold ---

When it is come that ye shall be unbound - ye shall see the wisdom of that which I have said unto thee -- for in no wise stall I let thee be overtaken by shadows of darkness -- Ye shall stand a living witness to My words - and ye shall be as My own apostle ---

For that have ye been called and ye shall give unto Me testimony of that which ye have become -- And ye shall know they oneness with thy Source - - Ye shall go into darkness no more -- Are ye not of a mind to seek that which shall unbind thee? Will ye not hear My Voice call unto thee?

I shall call unto each and every one which abides within the Earth -- For I am sent to deliver thee and ye shall not be overlooked -- For there are many sent to find thee and to be unto thee the way-shower -- They have gone before thee and they know the pit falls -- They have been unto thee thy hands and thy feet and they shall bring thee safely home ---

I Am the Path and the Light - I bring thee to the Gate and ye have but to open it -- The key has been given unto thee -- Ye have but to use it and ye shall be glad - and the Father shall be glad for long has He awaited thy return ----

And be ye of a mind to arise and come home - wherein is Peace and Joy -- For the first time I say unto thee that thy Mother Sara - which has given unto thee Her Love and protection thru thy pilgrimage within the Earth - shall come into the world of men made flesh -- She shall be unto thee mother and fellow being -- She shall give unto the world of men much Light - for She shall be known thruout the Earth for Her skill and for Love and strength -- She shall lift them up and She shall bring Peace unto the tortured - healing unto the sick and infirmed ---

So be ye alert for She shall walk among thee - and ye shall know Her - for She shall be the manifestation of perfection -- And so be it and Beleis ---

Blest are they which seek comprehension - for it shall be give unto them -- Blest are the hands which record My Words unto thee -- They shall know no sorrow - for I keep My Own - and I am unto them All things --- So be it that I shall come unto all that seek Me out and they shall be lifted up in the Name of the Father - Son and Holy Ghost - Amen ---

I AM thy Elder Brother – Sananda

Recorded by Sister Thedra of the Brotherhood of the Seven Rays –

Lake Titicaca - Peru - Bolivia --

Beloved ones who have asked for more Light: Our Blessed Lord and Director Sananda has asked me to tell you that I am now being prepared to come unto some of you which have received the "Sibors Portions" and are seeking the "Greater Part" - and it shall be in the time which is near -- And that there is Great Revelation in store for you -- And you shall be glad for your preparation -- I add my Love and Blessing to His ---

I am Sister Thedra of the Brotherhood of the Seven Rays --

40

Part #8

Beloved of My Being -- This is the day in which the One and only Gabriel shall come unto thee - and He shall give unto thee that which has been prepared for thee ---

It shall be sent unto them whose duty it is to send it out --

It shall be unto them much wisdom and Light ---

And so be it that ye shall be given a part which is prepared for thee by the One which calls Himself Masma --- Ye shall be unto Him His hands -- Ye shall have within thy hand the hand of One which has held the Earth upon his back -- He has been responsible for Her weight - Her width and Her breadth -- And now He speaketh that "they" may know Him -- He is both male and female - and He creates within Himself -- He has the Power of the Father - of which He is part - and which has sent Him Out -- For He has given unto the Earth of Himself that She may be brot into Her fullness and become the singing orb for which She was created ---

So be ye prepared for thy new part and it shall be for the good of All -- And so be it and Beleis ---

Beloved of Earth: Hear Me from afar - for I am in the 'Star Ship' whereupon I have spent much time -- And whereupon I am prepared to receive them which are to be brot within this place -- The same Star Ship which stood guard over Bethlehem on the night on which the One and Only Sananda was born unto Mother Mary - It was I - Gabriel - which came unto Her - as I now come unto another which is prepared to receive of the Father and of the Holy Ghost ---

41

And in the time which is near I shall stand upon the Earth as ye now stand -- I shall prepare some of thy fellow beings for an initiation within the Star Ship - and it shall be upon the Star Ship that the One which has within the hand the pen which records My words - I say unto thee ye shall be prepared for a new place and a new work ---

And in the time which is near there shall be prepared from among thee some which shall be taken unto the planet called Cerius - - Some shall go unto one called Clarion and others to Venus and Mars -- For this has the child of Earth awaited - for this age ---

And now it is the age of Light" ---

There shall be within the scope of every mans knowledge the One and only One Father of this Solar System -- And they shall have the knowledge of the Power which is invested within them - of Him ---

They shall no longer use the machinery which they have struggled to perfect -- They shall put the given power to work which is their inheritance - which has been dormant within them ---

When it is come that man has given his all for that which has availed him naught - he shall turn unto that Power which has created him and which has sustained him ---

Before thee is a Plan which shall mature in the Earth within the new dispensation ---

Ye shall be prepared for many new things - and much new experiences - and much wisdom shall be on thee bestowed ----

Be ye alert and see the "writing on the wall" for coming events cast their shadows before them ---

One which calls Himself Sananda has given unto thee of Himself for over one thousand years that ye be prepared for this time - when the veil of maya shall be removed -- And ye shall see that which exists beyond thy own limited horizon -- Will ye not be in thy place prepared to receive Us - which have guarded thee and directed thy progress within thy travail within the darkness? I have given unto thee of Myself - Of My Love and patience - that ye may come into thy inheritance ---

And ye shall awaken upon a morning not far off and find the world has passed out of berth unto another port -- there shall be great joy! For She shall shine in all Her Glory as a Sun made new -- She shall fulfill that for which She was created -- She shall become as a Sun unto another planet -- And She shall be as the home land of them which have fortuned unto themself such joy as She can give -- For this has the Earth been prepared -- And ye have been prepared to assist Her in time of need -- For it is given unto Her to be reborn - and there shall be birth pains - It is given unto thee to know that which shall occur and to hold Her steadfast within thy heart - to give Her of thy Love ---

Be ye not afraid for We which have held thee fast shall be at thy side -- And We shall be in the place wherein We are ready to rescue thee -- Many shall be brot out in the hour of disaster - It has been said - "there shall be much sorrow and suffering -- We come unto thee that ye shall not know suffering and sorrow -- We stand at thy side and admonish thee - see and hear! And be ye prepared for the time is near at hand -- Many stand upon the threshold of the Earth -

ready to release them which are prepared -- Be ye as one which knows the Truth and fear not! For We are with thee and We shall be unto thee thy hands and thy feet -- And they shall be swift and sure! ---

When ye are prepared - ye shall be prepared that ye might deliver others -- and therein is wisdom --- Be ye as wise as a "serpent" - and for thy part as wise as e fox - and ye shall be given that which can comprehend -- Ye shall be in no wise given that which shall be unto thee a bond - for We know no bondage - which are prepared to receive their freedom ---

When ye are given that which shall profit thee is it not wise to accept it? Blest are they which accept that which is proffered them -- For they shall be delivered of their bondage - and their freedom shall be given in wisdom and mercy ---

Blest shall ye be which give ear unto Us which hold thee within Our hearts and which await thy coming -- Ye shall receive more from this realm - and ye shall know that which has been kept for thee ---

I give thee my Blessings and My Light -- I am thy Servant in the service of the Most High - of which ye are part -- And be ye blest of the Father - Son and Holy Ghost - Amen ---

I am Gabriel of the Star Ship ---

Recorded by Sister Thedra of The Brotherhood of the Seven Rays –

Lake Titicaca -- Peru - Bolivia --

Part #9

Blest of My Being -- Be ye as the hands of the One which calls Himself Masma – And ye shall give it unto them whose duty it is to give it unto them which are seeking the Light and Wisdom - which shall be giver unto them which seek -- And so be it that Masma speaketh thru thy hand -- And so be it that it shall be blest by Him - --

Be on the whole blest - for I am the One which has gone the long way to bless thee -- And ye have in no wise heard My Voice nor seen My face - yet ye have been blest of My Presence -- For I have held upon My back the burden of thy planet Earth -- I have been responsible for Her growth - her weight and width since She was created -- and I have brot unto her surface warmth -- And I have caused the rivers to flow into the sea -- And I have given unto Earth the air which has sustained life therein -- I have given that which is necessary unto the soil for vegetation -- And I have given unto the Earth the power to produce after its kind -- And I have given unto the air the elements of cleanliness and unto the light rays power to purify -- And I have given unto the rose perfume of its own - and unto the lily its fragrance -- And in the fire element have I produced the fortune of the gnome -- And I have given unto the PORE the farthest reaches of feeling -- (And there is much to be said on that) -- For the pore is the most sensitive of all the creation of the Earth - - Ånd it is but the CASING for that which is called man -- And We which are of the Universal School - Who Know and See without limitation - know the Earth is an entity and ensouled within the Earth -- And is as one bound - even as ye are bound -- And ye have been prepared even as she is being prepared -- While it is in no wise the

45

greater part of her ministry unto thy solar system - it is indeed a great part -- For it is an age of great initiations thruout the Cosmos -- For Venus and all the planets within the galaxy are going thru a new place within the firmaments - and they are making ready their new berth - - And ye shall be made ready for thy new place of abode - and ye shall be within the place made ready -- I am responsible for the Earth's welfare -- I have given unto the hands of others that which shall be of help unto Me and unto the Earth -- There are the Ones which keep the tides -- And them which give unto air that it shall be purified - And them which give unto the cloud that rain might be a source of blessing -- And in thy language there are many helpers which are to be recognized -- And they all have given of Themself that the Earth might be blest - and in turn bless Her Children ---

In the time which is at hand ye shall come to know these Benefactors -- And ye shall pay homage unto them -- And ye shall give them recognition and love -- And will ye not give them credit for thy comfort? - And when it is come that ye shall have discomfort - will ye not call upon them - and will not be reminded of then? - Now I say unto thee that they shall have a new place and a new part - even as ye shall have ---

And ye shall rejoice that they too shall find freedom and Peace -- For it is decreed that Peace shall reign thruout the kingdom -- and this is the Plan from Earth's beginning -- And now it is said that the veil shall be removed - and so shall it be -- And ye shall see these which art thy Benefactors - and ye shall commune with them - and ye shall be as one which can comprehend Their language -- And They have the greatest knowledge of thine and thy Being -- Be as one which can comprehend that which is about thee - and that to which you pay little heed -- For without one of These would Earth loose her balance -- And Love is the Great Catalyst - the Great Balance -- And I ask thee to Love Her and pay Her due Homage in the Name of the Father - and the Son and the Holy Ghost ---

I AM Masma --

Recorded by Sister Thedra of the Brotherhood of the Seven Rays –

Lake Titicaca - Peru - Bolivia --

Part #10

Blest of My Being -- Will it not profit them to receive of the One and Only Archangel Michael -- For He has given much unto them - and He has gone the long way with them that they may be brot into the place wherein they shall have their freedom -- And be ye prepared to receive of Him and of the Father - Son and Holy Ghost -- So be it and Beleis ---

Beloved ones who are My sheep - and who have wandered upon the Earth - within her valleys and upon her hills – I come unto thee that ye might be made ready to receive in greater capacity that which is forth coming -- It has been said that a good shepherd knows his sheep and so he does -- And in the days ahead the sheep shall be gathered into the fold - and they shall be counted and numbered -- and there shall be none missing - for they shall all be found -- Are they not all in sight? ---

And do We the shepherds not know wherein they are? For We have been vigilant and true to Our trust -- And now wherein have I found My sheep sleeping? - when there are places wherein they may feed and rest - which surpasses any that they know ---

Will they not be brot out of their barren land into greener pasture - and will they not be better for the change?

And wherein have I said that they shall be without a fold? -- I have prepared a place wherein they may go - wherein the pasture is green and the water fresh and pure -- And wherein they may know security -- Blest are My sheep for I care for My own -- And I love them and protect them as ye protect the babe in arms -- I enfold them within My bosom -- and I give unto them of My Peace and of Myself -- Will they not remember their shepherd when the wolves approach? And will they not turn homeward? ---

For I am come unto them that they may be safely gathered in and that they may not be scattered -- Whereupon I have given of My love and of Myself -- I have given unto Myself - for it is my pleasure - My joy that My sheep are in their places -- and prepared for their new pasture -- And so shall they be ---

It is given unto Me to be upon the High Holy Mount -- I see wherein the danger lieth and the pitfalls -- And I bring them out of such snares and place them in safer places -- I am not so foolish as to be found asleep - for the wolves are about - and I keep constant watch -- Blest are they which know their shepherds - for they shall be gathered in and they shall know no sorrow -- Forget not that which I say unto thee within this parable - for I say unto thee that which ye can understand -- For ye are not schooled in the Higher places wherein All things are understood -- So I give unto thee that which is within the scope of the great and the small -- for it is indeed wise that they all know wherein they shall find comfort - and wherein they shall find their shepherd ---

On a hill not far away - shall stand One which has awaited His entrance -- And He shall call unto thee and ye shall hear Him -- And I say unto thee - heed the call and make haste unto Him and it shall profit thee - for He has been within the Earth for to bring thee out of the places of thy torment - and of thy hunger and longing -- Ye shall listen for the Voice - for He approaches and His footsteps are heard even now -- As I am in the place where in many shall be brot -- I are prepared to receive unto My place My Own - and I shall be glad to receive thee -- And wherein is it said that "there shall be many to receive thee and there shall be great joy and gladness!" ---

Some shall wait - some shall rush and some shall be unto themself traitor -- And they shall not hear nor shall they move out of their tracks -- Before thee is the plain and unadorned facts - And I wave neatly wrapped them and presented them unto thee -- Now ye shall do as ye will with them - for they are yours -- And I have given them unto thee with the hope that they shall profit thee - and be unto the food of much nourishment ---

And so be it that I shall await thy coming with much gladness and anticipation -- And remember wherein ye are comforted in the Name of One which has given unto Us Life and of His fortune -- I am thy Humble Shepherd Michael --

Recorded by Sister Thedra of The Brotherhood of the Seven Rays –

Lake Titicaca -- Peru - Bolivia –

50

Part #11

Beloved of My Being -- Now it shall be given unto thee to record that which shall be given unto 'them' by the beloved One which has given unto Us <u>so</u> <u>much</u> and is so little known in the world of men - Our One and only Solomena - and for Her have ye waited -- And ye shall be unto Her hand - and ye shall be blest of Her Presence and Her Wisdom -- And ye shall send it unto the whose duty it is to get it unto the ones who are to receive or her Words and Her Blessings -- And so be ye prepared to receive that which She has prepared for 'them' -- And thy portion shall be apart - and accept it with the blessing which goes with it - in the Name of the Most High -- And so be it and Beleis ---

Solomena

Beloved loved ones which I have held so dear and which is part of My Being -- I am in the place wherein All things are known - And I have kept constant watch over thy earthly progress - I have gone into the valleys with thee -- I have guided try footsteps that they should not stumble --- I have given thee wisdom which has brot thee thru the shadows -- And I have given unto thee faith that ye might lift up thine eyes -- I have given thee strength that ye might open them -- I have nursed thee when ye have fainted by the way -- I hope been unto thee thy shield and thy buckler in times of distress -- And I have led thee by thy hand wherein ye have found thy own flame - wherein it has burned upon the altar in the Inner Temple --

Ant ye have not remembered Me - in thy darkness for the shadows have overcast thy memory -- and ye have been in the place

51

wherein are the forces -- Yet the day is come when they darkness shall be dispelled - and ye shall know as ye are known --

We see not thy garments of flesh but the flame which burns within the eternal breast - and ye shall awaken unto that flame - And ye shall know thy self as ye are known ---

And ye shall be in the place wherein ye are prepared for that which shall be given unto thee - for it shall be given unto thee to be a spark fanned into a great flame which shall burn within the Temple of the Most High Living God -- And ye shall give unto the Father thy <u>thanks</u> <u>for</u> <u>thy</u> <u>Being</u> -- And ye shall give unto them which has held thee fast <u>thanks</u> <u>for</u> <u>thy</u> <u>well</u> <u>being</u> ---

Then ye shall be caused to know thy oneness with them which have been to thee all that ye have needed -- And from which have come all thy blessings and all the gracious ones which have held out a hand unto thee -- Be ye prepared to receive that which has been kept for thee for this age when ye shall be given comprehension which shall be unto thee thy deliverance from thy bondage - and from thy prison -- At no time has so many of other realms reached out unto thee that ye be lifted up as today -- It is time of much rejoicing in the realms wherein all things are known -- And such is My Work that ye may come to know them which have worked behind the veil and in silence -- Now that the veil is parted We shall step thru in wisdom - prudence! -- I have been called the "Goddess of Wisdom" and so I AM - and I shall not betray My Office - nor Myself - for I shall be true to My station – And I shall offer of wisdom and of My Love -- and I shall come unto thee as thou callest - and I shall be unto thee all that ye need -- Accept My Love and Service in the Name of the Most High which has sent thee out - and which shall bring thee back -- So be it according to the own will - and Selah ---

Blest are the hands which record My Words unto thee - And they have received Me in the Service of the Christ and of the Father -- And so be it they shall be lifted up -- And they shall know no sorrow -- Selah -- Solomena --

Recorded by Sister Thedra of the Emerald Cross –

Part #12

Blest of My Being -- I am in the place wherein is the One and only Osiris -- And He shall give thee that which shall be given unto 'them' which await more LIGHT from the higher realms ---

And He has prepared a part for 'them' and He gives it unto thee that they may receive it -- And it is given in the Name of The Father - Son and Holy Ghost -- So be it and Beleis ---

Osiris: -- Beloved ones whom I represent before the Throne of The Father -- I come at this time that ye may know no barriers - and that ye might have free communication with The Father ---

I bring unto thee a plan which shall be acceptable unto the children of the New Age -- And which shall break all barriers - and free thee from thy limitations - It is prepared and ready to be revealed unto them which are prepared for & New part" and a "New place" -- And when they are prepared - it shall be revealed unto them in its entirety -- For they which have been prepared shall be given an initiation in the Inner Temple of Osiris - and they shall have the wisdom of the wise and the prudence which is necessary for them which are to be initiated into the fullness of such a <u>plan</u> -- For it is given unto many to be prepared for that which is awaiting them -- And it is indeed wise to be prepared - for there is much in store for thee -- Be ye as "Wise as a Serpent and silent as a Sphinx " is one of the requisites for in the place wherein ye shall be prepared - ye shall be prepared in silence ---

And the <u>tongue</u> is thy pitfall - for it is not given unto the child of Earth to <u>master</u> the <u>tongue</u> - which is necessary for the Initiate --

And it is indeed wise to be as the Sphinx - for he has accumulated much knowledge by his <u>silence</u> -- And he is the Guardian of many mysteries -- And which shall be revealed unto the Initiate of the Inner Temple - which has presented himself worthy and ready at the gate ---

It is guarded by the Serpent which has the knowledge of the work within the Temple - and sees that none pass which are not worthy - And My part is to prepare thee to enter into the Inner Temple wherein is the Holy of Holies - and ye shall be one which has come alive -- And there shall be no more mystery - no more blindness - no more sorrow -- For ye shall stand as the Grand Master - and ye shall have within thy hand the rod which shall be made brass - and which shall be unto thee all power -- And ye shall be in the place wherein ye are prepared - for I have made Myself known unto thee for that purpose -- And I am indeed a porter for I stand at the gate and I pass only them with passports - and they which have the necessary credentials -- So be ye as wise as the Serpent and silent as the Sphinx - and <u>give</u> <u>thy</u> <u>attention</u> <u>unto</u> <u>thy</u> <u>own</u> <u>preparation</u> - for ye shall be called to account for every idle word - and every action which is not according to the law of <u>love</u> and <u>mercy</u> -- And ye shall face the Grand Master - and ye shall be as one which has poisoned thy own cup -- And so be it that ye shall find thy own way into the Inner Temple wherein I reside - and wherein I am prepared to receive thee - and I shall be glad to receive thee into the Holy of Holies in the LIGHT of the Christ - and in the Name of The Father - Son and Holy Ghost -- Amen --

I Am thy Brother in the service of The Most High - and so be it accorded unto thee as ye would have it -- I am Osiris - thy fortune unto the LIGHT of the Inner Temple ---

Recorded by Sister Thedra of the School of The Seven Rays –

Lake Titicaca - Peru - Bolivia ---

Blest of My Being -- It is indeed a privilege that our Brother has come unto Us - for many shall be lifted up thru Him - and by Him - - He has been in the place wherein all things are known and He knows whereof He speaks - He given unto them much wisdom and reveals nothing which is hidden - yet He draws them out - and gives into them that which should prepare them ---

And so be it that many shall be aware of His Presence and hear Him out - and so be it that it shall profit them - and blest shall they be -- And so be it and Beleis ---

Blest of My Being -- Ye shall have a part which has been prepared for thee by the One known as thy present Sibor Pearl - or as She is known within the place wherein I am - from the beginning of Her ministry - the Sister Nada - Who shall give unto "Them" a part -- And Who has gone the Royal Road -- And ye shall give it unto "Them"---

And ye shall add a footnote which I shall give unto thee and it shall suffice them -- And now ye shall have the part which She prepared for "Them" - And be ye blest of Her Presence - and so be it given unto thee in the Name of The Father - Son and Holy Ghost -- Amen ---

Sister Nada: -- Blest of My Presence -- I come unto thee who shall give My portion into My loved ones of the school of Earth ---

I am fortuned to be One of that school - but I have also been fortuned that the blessed Brothers and Sisters of LIGHT have reached out to Me a hand of mercy ----

And it was given unto Me to pass into the higher octaves without tasting death - for I had the Words of the blessed Master ever before Me: "And these things shall ye do - and even greater"-- And I have been unto My consciousness true - for as I have received of Him I have given unto others - for therein is the greatness of service -- And ye are told that death shall be the last enemy -- Now it is given unto many to go the Royal Road - whereupon there is only LIGHT - and they which enter that way wave not tasted death -- For they have gained their freedom from the wheel of rebirth - and they stand free forever -- And will ye not too partake of this freedom which is now offered unto thee? I am One of many Who are working to that end - that ye may have thy liberation ---

We Who are the Way Showers have come into thy consciousness for the part which has been held for this time ---

For never in the history of man has such great activity been activated within the realm of man -- And ye are fortunate to be part of the great dispensation which is now given unto thee -- And blest are We which are privileged to come unto thee to be part of it - and to be the Ones Who lend a hand -- Will ye not welcome Us and make Our work part of thy own? For We are separated only by a thin veil which shall be removed -- And ye have it within thy power to remove it -- Ye have but to ask - and to look up - and there shall be a great band of workers in the service of the great Divine Director at thy side ---

And ye shall have much given unto thee on that - in the near future -- And I ask of thee <u>patience</u> and <u>loyalty</u> unto thy own LIGHT - and to The Father which has given unto thee all that ye have need of - for He is unto thee all that ye shall ever need -- Give Him thy eternal <u>love</u> and praise and forget not that He is the SOURCE of thy Being - and unto Him ye shall return -- Now be ye as one which can see within thy own temple - the flame which burns within the Inner Temple - and upon the altar of The Living God -- And be ye blest of My Presence in the Name of The Living God - Our Father - Which has sent Us out and Which shall bring thee back -- I am thy Sister – NADA

Footnote: -- Blest of My Being -- There is a Sister of LIGHT Who has gone the Royal Road and She has profited thereby ---

For She now proffers thee a hand and stands free - and ready to assist thee even as I -- And I am come that the <u>way</u> might be made ready for Her - that ye might receive Her -- For I stand guard at the gate that none but the workers of Light might make their entrance into the port in which I am - and into which I come that ye may receive of the work of The Father -- I keep this port pure -- And ye shall receive much from this Source - in the Name of The Father - Son and Holy Ghost -- Amen -- So be it and Beleis ---

Recorded by Sister Thedra of The School of The Seven Rays –

Lake Titicaca - Peru - Bolivia --

Brother Bor Speaketh

Blessed Pioneer of the New Age - Be ye not dismayed for I have seen thy reward -- Ye know not how great it shall be!

For it is the beginning of thy search into new fields of learning -- Remember there were pioneers before thee -- Them which have given of themself that this age may come into being –

There was Lincoln - and there was Burroughs - and Wright too and Bell - Marconi and Edison and all the ones which have gone before thee –

I say unto thee -- Them which have betrayed themself have called them "crazy" ---

Be ye not dismayed for My hand is upon thee - and ye shall fear no man's scorn -- So be it ye shall walk as one made while - as one illumined -- So be it and Selah ---

I Am thy Sibor and thy Brother - Bor -

Recorded by Sister Thedra of The School of The Seven Rays --

Beloved -- Ye shall record that which I am now prepared to say unto thee - and it shall be for the good of all ---

For I say unto thee - many shall be without a place to lay their head -- They shall be as the fox without a burrow ---

I say unto thee - We - which have the greater vision - see and know - that which is nigh upon them - and they have been warned many times yet they have not prepared themself for this time - when they shall be brot face to face with their own folly - I say unto thee - they shall come to know what is meant by suffering ---

Not one - which <u>has</u> been warned - which <u>has</u> <u>not</u> prepared himself - shall be as ones brot out before disaster -- Yet all which have prepared themself - shall be brot out before the great and terrible day!

I say unto them - it is nigh upon them - when the energy which has been built up within the Earth - and about the Earth shall give forth - as it once did within the place wherein ye are (Tiahuanaco, Bolivia) - and which sent the great civilization and its hand-work into ruins - in the twinkling of an eye ---

So be it - that they which have ears to hear - let him hear - and let him be as one prepared ---

For it is now come when many have come into the Earth -- From three different planets have they come - that they may be prepared for this great day of sorrow! ---

I say unto thee - there shall be great sorrow and woe ---

So be it many stand ready to deliver them out before that day -- Now it is fortuned unto Me - to be One which has come from a far distant planet - that they may be prepared -- And yet - as for the greatest number - they have spat upon the <u>prophesies</u> which have been given to them - and they are yet in the dragons den -- And they are to be found in the places of gaming - and wherein they seek the pleasures of their own senses ---

I say unto them - it is nigh when they shall call out - and they shall say: "Lord! Lord! why have you allowed such as this to befall us?" ---

Now I say unto them - they have fortuned such unto themself - for it is but the energy of mans own mind - which he has sent out! ---

And he is fortuned now to be in embodiment - to reap that which he has sown thru past embodiments - so be it the LAW ---

Now I say unto them - it is the day of reckoning - the day of preparation -- All which turn unto the LIGHT - and seek his own Light - which is his own Divine - Eternal - indestructible Self - shall not know sorrow - for One shall be sent unto him - and he shall be as one prepared -- I say unto him - as he prepares himself so shall he receive -- And for this has many been sent into the Earth - of The Father Which has so WILLED it - that they all be brot out -- Yet has he not given unto them free will? - and not even The Father will trespass upon it ---

I say they shall prepare themself - and return unto Him - The Father - which has given unto them the precious gift of free will- of their own will ---

It is now come when this energy of which I speak - has built up within the Earth and within the Ether - so that at any time it could give forth -- And it is said unto thee again - many billions of tons of energy is stored in the Earth - Along the coast of both the Americas - and far into the ocean to the west ---

I say unto thee - not one particle of the Earth's surface shall remain as it is at present -- So be it that it shall undergo a great change in its interior - as on the surface ---

Within the greatest of all nations - the waters shall flow into the interior - and it shall recede in a short while - yet a great mountain range shall be thrown up - within the east of the great Rocky Mountains -- Great rivers shall flow in the deserts wherein there are no waters - and great animals from the sea shall be left upon the land to torment them which are fortuned to survive - and they shall know much torment and woe ---

I have said unto thee many times - the day of sorrow is nigh upon them - now it is even nearer ---

And they which think themself wise - shall be confronted with their own foolishness and they shall be as traitors ---

I say again: "There are none so foolish as he which thinks himself wise - and none so sad as he which betrays himself" -- So be it a great truth indeed -- I have again come unto thee that they may receive these - My Words unto them -- And I say unto thee - these My Words shall go out into the lands - and they shall again be warned -- And they shall again be as ones which spit upon the prophecies - and again they shall say: "Oh - we have heard that for years"-- I say unto them - "Ye fools- have ye not the mind to comprehend this - that ye are warned in advance - that ye should be warned - before being destroyed?" I say unto thee ye have been warned - and warned again - and ye have turned a deaf ear -- Ye stand as ones with feet of lead -- Ye have not turned unto thy Source of Being for thy salvation - nor have ye sought help from the Realms of LIGHT -- So be it that ye shall be as ones which have thrown overboard thy own life-belt ---

Now hear Me in this - for I am of a mind that ye shall hear - and no more can I do - for it is for thee to choose ---

Now it is said that "Ye may be destroyed"-- Yet I say unto thee -- That which is Eternal - and which is given unto thee of God The Father - is indestructible -- Yet when one loses his atomic vehicle (or his body) in a catastrophe such as this of which I speak - he is thrown into panic - into the greatest of torment - and he is in this state for a prolonged time -- Now heed ye this - death - or so-called death - is not the end - for woe unto him which goes into panic -- So be ye as ones true unto thyself - and ye shall be given assistance from the higher realms -- So be it and Selah -- And for this have I come unto thee - that ye may be delivered out - So be it - Amen and Selah ---

I Am One which has been sent of God The Father -- I Am Tephani - Of The Temple of Tau - The Temple of Osiris - and The Temple of LIGHT -- So be it - Amen ---

Recorded by one which I have appointed - Sister Thedra

A Message from Tephus to The World

Beloved of My Being -- I now command thee to record that which I am about to say unto thee - and it shall be for the good of all ---

And it shall be sent out unto all which have been appointed the porters of Law and Justice - And which have set themself up as the defenders of Truth and Justice ---

I say unto thee: "They which have set <u>themself</u> up as the defenders of Truth and Justice"...

And they which reject My Words - and which spit upon them - shall be brot to account for their foolishness -

Now it is come when there shall be much action within the realm of man - and he shall be as the ant which has been displaced - he shall run hither and yon -- He shall be at a loss for words - he shall not know which way to go ---

For it is now come when great restlessness shall come upon him - and he shall seek of man - the solution ---

Yet I say unto him - that he shall find no solution in the realm of man - for it is given unto man- to be yet in darkness --

I say unto him - the Earth and man - is going thru great initiations - and the Earth is passing thru the dark and dangerous parts of the firmaments ---

And it is with the greatest wisdom and skill - that is bestowed upon the Guardians of thy planetary system that She - the Earth is kept within Her orbit ---

Now ye which are of the Earth - have no concept of the magnitude of thy Solar System or of the work of the Guardians thereof ---

I say unto thee - ye are as little children playing with high explosives which ye know nothing of ---

Now hear Me in this - and be ye as ones forewarned - for I am come unto thee from out of the Realms of LIGHT -- wherein these LAWS are known - and wherein We see and know that which ye have fortuned unto thyself -- For We the Guardians - have been sent unto the Earth that ye may not destroy thy physical self ---

I say - "That ye may not destroy thy physical self" ---

Now be ye mindful of this - that they which are the traitors shall know much suffering and torment - and ye shall be as ones which call out - and ye shall say: "Lord! Lord! where art thou - have ye forsaken us? "---

And I say unto thee - ye shall be as ones which have thrown overboard thy own life belt ---

Now be ye as ones true unto thyself - and heed My Words - and ye shall be given great assistance from the higher realms ---

And there are many now within the Earth - from out the Realms of LIGHT for the purpose of giving thee assistance ---

Now when ye have been prepared to receive Us - We shall make Ourself known unto thee - and ye shall know Us - and ye shall be made glad! So be it and Selah ---

Now ye shall be of a mind to receive Us - and of a mind to learn - and as ye are prepared so shall ye receive --

Now ye shall be as ones prepared - for great revelation shall be given unto them which are prepared to receive it ---

Now hear me - for I am come that ye may be prepared for the great learning - the great revelation --

And when ye are of a mind to receive Us - One shall come unto thee - and give unto thee as ye are prepared to receive ---

Now I say unto thee: "There are none so foolish as he which thinks himself wise - and none so sad as he which betrays himself"

Now be ye as ones true into thyself - and give unto Me credence - and I shall give unto thee the part which has been kept for thee for this day ---

Now it is come when they which have prepared themself shall be brot out of darkness ---

And <u>new</u> <u>laws</u> shall be revealed unto them - and <u>new</u> <u>places</u> shall be opened up unto them which is prepared for such revelation---

Now I say unto thee - they which prepare themself for such revelation - shall overcome the law of gravity - and the law of attraction -- He shall be one with the <u>law</u> of Being - and the law of elements shall be revealed unto him -- So de it and Selah ---

Now ye have but to turn unto thy own Source of Being - and ask The Father for thy release from bondage - and ye shall be heard and answered ---

Now I say unto thee - ye shall seek thy own Eternal LIGHT - thy own Divine Self - which is the Christ - and ye shall be as one brot out of darkness - and ye shall find that which has been hidden from thee shall be revealed unto thee -- So be it in the Name of The Most High Living God -- Amen and Selah ---

I am One sent of God The Father - that ye may have LIGHT - and that ye may not know sorrow ---

I Am Tephus - of The Temple of Tau - Osiris - and of The Temple of Light -- So be it and Selah ---

Recorded by My Porter which is appointed by The Federation of Brotherhoods -- Sister Thedra --

Beloved of My Being -- I shall add My part unto that of Our Beloved Guardian - Which has come unto the Earth from out the Temple of Tau - and Osiris - that ye may not know sorrow--

Now it is come when the doors of other worlds- other realms - other planets - shall swing wide before thee -- Yet I say unto thee ye shall prepare thyself to enter therein - for none shall enter therein unprepared - And for that has The Father seen fit to give unto thee a new dispensation and a new order ---

Now I say unto thee - ye are of a new order - and ye have been given a new dispensation that ye may now return unto Him - and be made whole ---

I say unto thee - it is now the day of salvation - when ye may be brot out of darkness and bondage forever -- And for that has many been sent of The Father - even as I am sent - that ye may have thy inheritance which The Father has WILLED unto thee ---

So be it HE The Father - has seen fit to send many into the Earth at this time - that ye may find thy own Light - which ye thyself have hidden - when ye went into the world of darkness of thy own free will ---

Now ye shall return unto Him of thy own will - and He shall be glad --- Now hear me out - for I am come that ye may awaken from thy sleep - and from thy lethargy - and ye shall be glad ---

Now ye shall prepare thyself to receive the greater part - and for that have I come into the Earth - that ye may be prepared to return unto the Source of thy Being and be made whole -- So be it and Selah ---

I am He which is sent that ye may be brot out from the Earth - that ye may be given thy freedom from bondage - that ye may have thy own inheritance in full - which is thy Godhood – So be it and Selah ---

I Am The Son of God The Father - which was born of Mary - and the ward of Joseph -- now known in the Inner Temple as - Sananda

Now ye shall copy and send it unto each of the Porters which have been appointed the Guardians of Truth and Justice - and they shall be responsible for its circulation -- So be it and Selah --- Bor - -

Recorded by Sister Thedra of The School of The Seven Rays

Note: - Brother Bor - is one of the Kumaras - and One of the Twentyfour Elders -- Thedra –

68

Part #13

Blest of My Being -- Be ye prepared for a part which shall be given unto them of the One and only Child of the great and powerful Posied - for it shall be given unto Him to give unto thee a part which He has kept for thee for this day - and it shall be given in the Name of The Father - Son and Holy Ghost -- Amen -- And it shall be sent unto them - whose duty it is to get it unto them which are prepared to receive of His Words -- And so be it that they shall be blest - and they shall be prepared to receive in greater capacity -- And so be it and Beleis--

Beautealu - Son of The Posied

Be ye of the Earth blest of My Presence -- For I am come unto thee - that the way may be prepared to receive My Father The Posied - Which has within him the power of The Father and The Son and the Holy Ghost -- He has given of Himself that this age may come into its own -- Wherein is it recorded that He shall return unto the new land? - which shall be as the lotus now is -- For as the lotus now is - so too shall the land which is America of the North become - and as She now is - so too shall the lotus become -- And with that be ye foretold of the future events - which shall be unto thee a forewarning -- And ye shall be prepared for the change which shall come about thru natural law - which is given unto Us to understand -- Wherein have ye prepared thyself for the portion which shall be given unto thee? For many are coming into the world of men - and they are giving into thee that which shall prepare thee - for the world which ye shall come to know - which is but the beginning -- For ye shall be given the mind to comprehend that which ye have not even dreamed of -- For ye shall be awakened unto that which lies beyond thy present limited horizon - and beyond thy present conception and understanding ---

Ye shall be put into a place which has been prepared - and - which shall be unto thee new -- And ye shall go in as a prepared people - for in no wise shall ye enter unprepared - each one shall be in his own environment -- And it shall be wise to improve thy environment - for ye shall see the wisdom of that --We which have been in the places which are beyond thy conception - and within the places which he know not - have been prepared to come unto the Earth - that She might be made new - and fulfill Her destiny - as the other planets within the Solar System shall too fulfill theirs---

By the time ye are prepared - the Earth shall be ready - and ye shall be put into the proper places -- And the Earth shall be free for Her new part - as it is ordained that She shall undergo many changes - and She shall have a rest period -- Then ye may be prepared to share in Her glory - for She shall be as a Sun - and She shall be as one made new -- Be ye as the wise and give ear into Me -- For I have been in these places and I know whereof I speak - for I have read the records of the Earth - and the heavens - And I have comprehension of the laws which govern them ---

And ye shall be given all that ye can comprehend -- Ye shall be in the Earth prepared for thy new place -- And there are many places - and each unto his own -- Be ye fortuned that which ye have prepared for thyself - for ye have prepared thyself for thy place - and thy place is prepared for thee - according unto thy own preparation as ye would have it -- From the beginning of the age which began with the sinking of the lotus - it has been the fortune of the new land to be the <u>Light</u> of the world - the hope of many which have sought Her protection as a refuge -- And within this age She shall fulfill that for which she is destined ----

She shall dip into the waters - as one baptized - and She shall again arise refreshed and purified - as the lotus shall arise in all her glory - and which shall be new and fresh - as the garden of the new age -- It is given unto Me and My Father The Posied - to prepare the lotus for a new habitation - and a new part which shall bless her as never the old did - and that is saying much - for it was a great age for her ---

And she has rested - and now she shall come into her fullness -- Be it such as shall come unto the land which We have prepared for a new part and a new part shall be given unto much of the Earth's surface which shall be changed and made new -- Be ye forewarned and fore-prepared - for it is planned from the beginning - and it shall be given unto her to fill the plan - We Who have watched the foregone events of the Earth have known that which shall come and the consequences which shall follow -- And We have worked with the children of Earth that they shall know as little discomfort as possible - and for that have I given this unto thee -- I shall come unto thee and give thee that which ye are prepared to understand -- For as ye reach out - much knowledge shall be given into thee - and greater capacity for comprehending that which many shall give unto thee -- And it shall be given unto thee with <u>wisdom</u> and <u>prudence</u> -- And so be it as ye would have it - for none shall give thee more than ye can receive ---

Be ye forewarned and forearmed --

And be ye blest of Our Presence - and Our help -- I am at thy service in the Name of The Father - and of the New Dispensation---

And so be it that ye shall be prepared to receive thy inheritance ---

I am thy Elder Brother - Beautealu - Son of The Posied --- ·

Recorded by Sister Thedra - School of The Seven Rays --

Blest of My Being -- Ye shall now be prepared to receive that which is prepared for 'them' which are prepared to receive the Words of the Father of Beautealu - The Posied -- And ye shall be in thy place prepared to receive the Posied - for He shall come unto thee and He shall give thee instructions in thy new part which has been kept for thee - and which has been prepared for thee -- And so be it given unto thee in the Name of The Father Son and Holy Ghost - and so be it and Beleis ---

The Posied: -- Be ye blest of My Presence and of My Being - I Am the Posied - and I am come unto thee that ye may have greater comprehension and more wisdom -- For I am prepared within the place wherein I am - to be of much help unto thee at this time -- I have been schooled within the land of the lotus - and I have been initiated in the Temple of Osiris -- And it is given unto Me to have the understanding which is of The Father - and the discernment which is given unto the Initiate of Osiris -- And ye shall partake of that which I have learned when ye are prepared - for that do ye not wait -- And ye shall prepare thyself for that which I am prepared to give unto thee - for I am come that ye may be prepared for thy place which is prepared -- And ye shall be given that which shall be unto thee thy deliverance from much sorrow and much suffering -- I Am that for which I have been prepared - and ye too shall become that for which ye shall be prepared - And now ye shall begin thy search into thy new part and into that which has been kept for this time -- For it has been given unto Me - The Posied to prepare the lotus for a new habitation - and the habitation shall be prepared for the lotus -- And ye shall prepare thyself to be put into a new place wherein are many which await thy coming - which shall be unto thee Sibors - and They shall give into thee that which has been kept for thee - and that which shall be unto thee that which ye shall have need of -- For it is given unto Them to know the law of the losoloes - and They shall give unto thee of Their wisdom and understanding -. So be it that many shall come unto thee to prepare thee for that which shall be given unto thee - and so be it and Beleis ---

Wherein is it said that ye shall awaken unto a new world? And so shall ye awaken unto many new worlds -- For it is given unto Me to be of many worlds - guest- and they have received Me as they shall receive them which are prepared to enter into other worlds - other planets -- And in no wise shall ye pass the great barrier unprepared -- And so be ye prepared in love and wisdom - for I am in the Secret Place of the Most High wherein I am prepared to receive unto Myself them which are prepared -- And so may ye be prepared to enter in --

And so be it given unto Me to come unto thee as One which has gone the Royal Road -- And therein shall be great joy and much gladness - so be it accorded unto thee -- And in the Name of The Most High - shall I come unto thee again and again -- I AM thy

Brother in The LIGHT of The Christ and so be it that ye shall walk therein ---

The Posied - of The Emerald Cross

Recorded by Sister Thedra - Brotherhood of The Emerald Cross

Part #14

Blest of My Being -- Be ye prepared to receive a part which is prepared for thee by the one known as "The Worthy Grand Master" of the Inner Temple -- For from Him comes great wisdom - and they which receive of Him shall be richly blest -- I bow unto Him and I give unto Him the greatest respect - for He is in the place wherein all things are known - and He has gone the way of the Royal Road - - And He has been unto the Earth a source of much LIGHT - and He shall be in the Earth made known to men - and for that does He now give unto thee that which He has kept for 'them' -- And it shall be but the beginning of His Revelation - for He has much for them which are of a mind to receive of Him -- And so be it that they shall profit thereby - and so be it and Beleis -- Be ye at peace - and prepare thyself for thy rest which the pore needs - and in the day ahead ye shall receive that which is promised thee -- So be it and Beleis ---

Blest of My Being -- Will it not profit 'them' to receive of The Grand Master? for He is the manifestation of all that which we shall become -- It is given unto Him to be the Father of perfection-- He stands within the LIGHT of The Christ made manifest - that we may have the contact with The Father thru Him -And wherein is it said that the Grand Master shall reveal Himself in the Inner Temple? and so shall He - and with the power which is invested within Him of The Father - He is all powerful -- And He has the wisdom and the prudence befitting His Office - And it shall profit them to receive Him and of Him - So be it and Beleis. ---

Most Worthy Grand Master

Blest of My Being -- I reveal Myself unto them which are prepared to enter the Inner Temple -- And for that have I prepared a PLAN - and it shall be fortuned into each and every one which seeks admittance - and diligently prepares themself to be brot into the Temple wherein I am -- I have waited long for thy preparation - and there has been many sent out to bring thee in - ye heard not the call -- The time is come that ye shall be cured of thy deafness and of thy drunkenness - and ye shall alert thyself - and ye shall be as one come alive - for ye have slept overtime -- I am prepared for this day - and I am prepared to awaken thee! For in no wise shall I deliver My own unto the power of the black dragon which lies in wait -- I have prepared a portion which shall be given unto thee - and it shall be "bitter" -- And as ye have given unto <u>thyself</u> that which ye have called "sweet" - ye will find My portion very "bitter" Yet when ye have drunk of it thy stomach shall be sweetened - and ye shall become new - and ye shall be reborn - and ye shall walk with equilibrium - and ye shall lose it no more -- For that which I have prepared for thee is the better part of wisdom - and ye shall remember thy Being - which was before thy going out into darkness - when ye was with The Father and The Mother perfect ---

And We which have not separated Ourself form them - and Who are with them - are in the Inner Temple prepared to receive tree - and ye shall be prepared to enter -- It is the better part of wisdom to prepare thyself - for there are many which stand ready to groom thee for thy new part - which shall be given unto thee of The Father Whom I represent unto thee --

And so be ye fortuned that which ye fortune unto thyself -- "As a man asketh so it is portioned out unto him" - - And as ye calleth out ye are answered -- And ye shall be as one which has within thy hand the "KEY" to the door -- Ye have but to turn the key - and the door shall swing wide before thee -- Blest are they which turn the key - for I shall reveal unto them all things which have mystified them - and there shall be no more mysteries - and suffering - no more darkness wherein is thy suffering and mystery -- Be ye as wise as a Serpent - and silent as a Sphinx -- Give unto thyself that which I have allotted unto thee - and ye shall profit much -- I shall be unto thee all that which ye shall need and more!

Ye have but to apply thyself - and seek the LIGHT which is within thy own port- and it shall be revealed unto thee in all its brilliance -- So be it accorded unto thee as ye would have it - in the Name of The Father Which has sent thee out and Which shall bring thee back -- I am He which guards the LIGHT on the Altar of the Inner Temple - known only as The Grand Master ---

Recorded by Sister Thedra - Brotherhood of The Emerald Cross

Blest of My Being -- Ye shall now receive that which Beautealu has prepared for "them" - and it shall profit them -- And so be it and Beleis ---

Beautealu: -- Blest of My Presence -- Say unto them which are to receive My Words: "That they shall hear me out" - for I am come unto them that they shall hear! - and that they shall comprehend what they hear -- For in the time which is near they shall be caught up short - and they which have not heeded that which is said unto them shall be given much torment -- And them which give heed shall be prepared to be delivered from that which would be unto them torment -- It has been said over and over again and again Prepare thyself - for the day approaches swiftly when ye shall be removed from the surface of the Earth! - and will ye not heed the cry which has gone out? - and which shall be heard thruout the Earth -- "Prepare thyself! Prepare thyself!" shall ring thruout all the Earth! And ye who have feet of lead shall be found within thy tracks unprepared! - and I say unto thee: "Sad indeed shall be he which is found wanting" -- Behold! I stand ready to be unto thee hand and foot --Ye have but to seek Me out and I shall come unto thee - and I shall give unto thee that which ye shall need for thy preparation - and for thy own salvation -- And be ye not misled - for "There are none so foolish as them which think themself wise!" -- I have given thee much within this portion - if ye but see it - and if ye but accept it -- And so be it as ye would have it - and be it unto thee according to thy own will ---

I AM the Son of The Posied -- Beautealu -- School of The Seven Rays ---

Recorded by Sister Thedra - School of The Seven Rays

Part #15

Blest of My Being - - It is given unto Me to give unto thee that which has been kept for thee - that for which ye have waited -- And now be it given unto thee in the Name of The Father - Son and Holy Ghost -- Amen ---

Blest of My Being -- I Am thy Father - and I AM thy Mother - for the two are ONE - and I AM That Which ye shall become -- For it is given unto thee to return unto Me and be made whole - I shall bring thee back - and I shall be unto thee <u>that</u> for which ye were created ---

I shall give unto thee power to control the elements - and the power to create - and the power to give LIFE unto the dead -- And I shall give unto thee a new body - and I shall give unto thee that which has been kept for thee -- And ye shall go out unto them - which are of the world and ye shall give unto them as I give unto thee ---

And ye shall lift them up - and ye shall be unto them all that they need -- And they shall be prepared for a new part - and ye shall be My hands made manifest -- And I shall invest within thee the power to heal their infirmities - and their blindness ---

And ye shall go into all the world - and ye shall give "them" that which I shall give unto thee for "them"-- And so be ye prepared for thy new part - and it shall be given unto thee in My Name - and in the Eternal Verities: -- And whereupon is it written that ye shall be the hands of Mother Sara made manifest?

So be it and Beleis ---

I AM HE Which has given unto thee thy Being - and I shall be unto thee that which ye shall become -- And so be it and Beleis ---

Sananda: -- Blest of My Being - Will it not profit "them" to receive of Me - that which is given unto Me of My Father? -- I have kept a portion for "them" - and it shall be given unto them in the Name of The Father - Son and Holy Ghost ---

Beloved ones who are My sheep - I have kept this portion for thee - and now I shall give it unto thee with My blessing - and ye shall receive it in the Name of The Father Son and holy Ghost ---

Wherein have I said - "I shall go to prepare a place for thee?" And so I did! And it is ready - and will ye refuse it - or shall ye accept it? - for it is given unto thee to have free will -- And it is My part unto thee - to point the <u>way</u> which is prepared before thee - and ye shall be given thy choice - yet many shall come unto thee that ye may make a wise choice ---

Be ye wise - and give unto The Father thyself - and thy will -- And HE shall be unto thee all that ye shall ever need -- Ye shall have the wisdom of the Sphinx - and the power of the Posied -- Ye shall be as one come alive - and ye shall have thy head unbound - and ye shall see and hear as one unbound -- For it is given unto Me that I shall walk among thee - and I shall seek out them which ask of Me - and I shall prepare them for a part which has been kept for them - a part which shall be part of their inheritance - and given unto them in the beginning ---

Yet it is within thy power to receive it or reject it -- Ye have only to ask and it shall be given unto thee - and ye are wise indeed to ask - for it shall profit thee much -- Will ye not lift up thine eyes unto thy Source - and give thanks for thy Being? And ye shall have the greatest blessing which can be bestowed upon thee -- Ye shall come to know thy oneness with The Father - and that which has been portioned unto thee by HIM -- Ye shall be in no wise bound by HIM for HE has given unto the freedom --And forget not that ye are bound by the legirons which ye have forged thyself -- And when ye ask and seek the LIGHT which never fails - thy legirons shall be cut away - and ye shall know no bondage -- I have said: "I shall be thy bondsman" - so shall I -- I stand ready to set thee free - and ye shall be wise to accept My offer - wherein can ye lose? Blest are they who ask - for they are heard - and answered ---

No plea is overlooked - for I am alert unto thy calls and thy needs -- Be ye prepared to receive Me - for I shall make Myself known unto them which seek Me out - and they shall be given comprehension to understand that which I say unto them -- Will it so and I shall be with thee - and I shall be unto thee all that ye shall need -- I Am at thy service in love and wisdom - and in the Name of The Father - Son and Holy Ghost ---

Sananda -- School of The Seven Rays –

Recorded by Sister Thedra - School of The Seven Rays

Blest of My Being -- Will it not profit "them" to have that which has been prepared for them? -- There is One which has come unto thee - which has prepared a part for them - and it shall provide them much nourishment and food for thot -- And wherein have I said - "There is no value in thinking?" - it is best to <u>know</u>! -- And ye shall know - and it shall be given unto all to know - and to know that they know! - therein is <u>wisdom</u> - Be ye as the hand of Him which stands ready to give unto them that which is prepared for them by Our Brother of LIGHT - One which is known as " Muru - and Whose <u>new</u> <u>name</u> is <u>Maheru</u> -- Wherein is it said that He has gone unto another place of abode? - and so He has - and the New Name shall indicate as much -- And so be ye blest of His part - and may it bless all which shall receive it in the Name of The Father - Son and Holy Ghost -- Amen ---

Maheru: -- Beloved of the School of Earth -- I Am come unto thee in the Name of the One Which has sent Us out - and the One Which now calls thee home -- It has been given unto Me to complete My mission in the Earth and return unto The Father ---

I have given much time unto the Earth - and the "wayfarers" therein -- And I know wherein are the valleys and the mountains -- I know thy shortcomings - I know thy strength - and from whence It cometh -- I am now in the place wherein I am prepared to assist thee in greater measure - for I am not bound by the limitations of the laws of the Earth - and I am not of the Earth -- For that has it been given unto Me to become <u>One</u> with The Father - and to be as HE IS - which is <u>everyone's</u> inheritance -- Will ye not accept thy inheritance which is offered into thee at this time? I have held out a hand unto thee - and ye have but to take that which is for thee - and ye shall be glad -- Be ye as on which can know the TRUTH which shall set thee free -- When it was given unto Me to come into the place wherein I am - I could not speak for the joy - it knew no bounds! -- And I said: "This shall be given unto every child of Earth to know such joy!" -- And then I vowed that I should not rest until everyone shared the same joy and knew such glory! ---

And I shall praise The Father thruout all Eternity for HIS <u>Mercy</u> and Wisdom ---

My mission is <u>not</u> <u>complete</u> - for I have given unto the children of the Earth my love and My fortune - which was given unto Me of The Father - and now <u>I</u> <u>pledge</u> <u>Myself</u> <u>anew</u> that I shall not rest until everyone is delivered up - and on the planes of New Jerusalem -- "And were it not so I would have told thee" -- Remember these words? And were it not so I would not tell thee -- For I am come unto them which are to receive My Words - and which are to receive of My <u>love</u> and My <u>teaching</u> -- I am in the ministry of The Christ for a long time - and I have had much experience with thee - and I know the <u>longing</u> of the human heart -- I too know thy sluggishness and thy failures -- But I say unto thee: "Bestir thyself - shake off thy sluggishness - and give ear unto Them which are standing near and calling out unto thee" - for it shall stand thee "four square" - and ye shall have need of balance and strength -- Ye shall partake of My strength and knowledge if ye will - for it is offered in the Name of The Most High - and ye shall profit thereby ----

I AM thy Older Brother -- Maheru -- Brotherhood of The Seven Rays ---

Recorded by Sister Thedra - Brotherhood of The Seven Rays

Lake Titicaca -- Bolivia - Peru –

83

Part #16

Blest of My Being: Ye shall be given a part which is different from the rest - for it shall be given unto thee of The Father - and He shall give unto 'them' which has been hidden - and which has been kept for this time -- Ye shall be unto Him His hands made manifest for that which is to be given unto 'them' -- And so be it and Beleis ---

The Father

Be ye as ones which has separated thyself from Me -- And ye shall return unto Me - for I am within the place wherein I am prepared to receive thee -- There has been given unto the Earth a New Dispensation whereby ye may return unto Me without having thy own form of Earth changed -- For ye shall be given the power to change it at will -- Them which abide within the place wherein I am - are prepared to give thee all that ye need for thy present preparation that ye may be brought into the place wherein I am ---

And I have given unto them the power to bring thee in -- And as ye have been given free will - it is wise to use it for thy own salvation ---

I am not given to preachments - yet I say I have sent My Emissaries unto thee with My Plan which shall be fulfilled - that ye may have that which is thy inheritance -- I have willed it that all which have separated themself from Me return unto Me -- So be it -- And be ye prepared for that which shall be allotted unto thee -- Were it not that ye were given free will in the beginning I should pick thee up and give thee as a mother a wayward child - My Love and Blessing -- What would that profit thee? As the seed within the

84

pod ye shall ripen and come forth of thy own accord -- For from the beginning of thy sojourn within the Earth have I awaited thy return -- Many have returned unto Me the wiser and the better for their experience - and will it not be so with thee? As ye have sown so have ye reaped and now the harvest is over - and ye shall be gathered in as the sheaves from the field ---

And ye shall be as a child of darkness no more -- I am glad the day of thy deliverance is come and for that have I waited -- Before thee is a plan which has been fashioned within the Inner Temple - and it is given to them which I have sent unto thee to reveal unto them which are to bring it into fulfillment -- And many shall be prepared to be my hands and feet -- For I shall invest within them My power - and I shall cause them to remember their oneness with Me - and foretake of My Wisdom - My Power - My Love - And so be it unto thee as ye would have it - in My Name ---

And as I have given unto thee or Myself - I shall be unto thee all that ye shall need -- I Am thy Father - within the secret place of The Most High - and so be it ye shall abide with Me forever --- Recorded by Sister Thedra ---

Sananda

Beloved ones - who are My sheep: Wherein have I said: "I shall come again to claim My own" - and so shall I - for I am among thee that ye may know Me -- And I have given thee of my Love and of Myself that ye might know Me -- Yet ye are not awakened and will ye not stir thyself - for the time is come that ye shall call - and ye shall be as one which has thrown thy life-belt overboard! For ye are in no wise prepared for that which ye shall encounter ---

I have given then that which should prepare thee - yet ye slumber - and ye have not stirred in thy slumbers ---

Will ye not be up and about thy preparation? for the day draweth nigh when ye shall say: Lord! Lord! deliver us! - and ye shall be as one which hangs by his toes! Be ye wise and hear Us Who are the ones which can see from the High places - and We know what lies before thee -- And ye are in the valley wherein it is dark - and ye see not which we see ---

We have given of Our Wisdom and of Ourself that ye may be lifted up -- Will it not profit thee to stand still and hear Us out? For it is given unto Us to give unto thee that which is given unto Us of The Father ---

And ye shall be prepared -- And so be it the wise way - for We have come that ye be prepared (PPP) and ye shall! Yet ye have thy choice of two ways - one is the Royal Road - one is the way of the flesh -- And them which choose the Royal Road - shall not taste death for they shall be resurrected even as I - and they shall stand forth in all their glory made whole -- And they shall be as God The Father - and they shall be as one with Him - and they shall know no more suffering and sorrow ---

So be ye given a foretaste of thy inheritance -- And it shall be given unto many to be resurrected and to be free from the gravitation of the Earth - and the attraction of the moon -- They shall be free even as We - which have gone the 'Royal Road' and they shall know no bondage - for they shall have 'Light bodies' and they shall control them - even as they shall control the Elements -- And that which is part of thy inheritance have I given unto thee -- So be ye blest of My

Presence - and be ye of a mind to receive of Me and of the Workers in the Light of The Christ - and of The Father which has sent thee out - and Which shall bring thee back ---

I Am thy Elder Brother Sananda - Brotherhood of The Emerald Cross --- Recorded by Sister Thedra - Brotherhood of The Emerald Cross ---

Blest of My Being: Will it not profit them to receive of the one and only Poseid? He shall give unto them the part which has been kept for them -- And it shall be given in the Name of The Father - Son and Holy Ghost - Amen -- Be ye as the hand of Him made manifest that they may receive His Words - and ye shall be blest of His Presence - and so be it and Beleis ---

The Poseid

Blest ones of Earth: Be ye blest of My Being - and be ye blest of The Father - for I am come unto thee that ye might have great knowledge of Him - and of the ones Which are with Him - which have not separated themself from Him -- Be ye of a mind to comprehend these things - for it is the order of the day that each one be given all the Truth - and not in part ---

It is a big order - yet ye shall be prepared to learn - and ye shall be given all that ye are capable of consuming ---

While it is the law that ye shall be in a new place - ye have the choice of places - for as ye are prepared ye are fortuned thy place -- And as ye ask of The Father of Us for more Light - many are sent unto thee that ye might be prepared for a place within the higher realms ---

And ye shall be given all that ye can comprehend -- For it is long that ye have been in bondage - and thy capacity for Light is small - for that have I revealed Myself unto thee that it may be increased -- And for that are many revealing Themself at this time -- <u>Wherein have ye prepared thyself for the day of revelation</u> wherein all things shall be made clear? - and wherein all things shall be known -- Ye are fortuned to be part of the Greatest Age which has come unto the Earth! -- And forget not that ye have been part of many ages -- Yet thy memory has been covered - and it shall be uncovered! - and ye shall remember as ye are remembered by Them which are thy Sibors ---

They which sibor thee have a continuous memory - and they are prepared to give unto thee a Portion which shall break thy bond - and ye shall be free as ye have not known freedom since thy going out from The Father ---

Yet ye shall return unto Him - and ye shall have thy head unbound - and ye shall remember that which ye have said in thy sleep - and that which has been blanked from thy memory shall be clear before thee ---

Wherein is it said that 'the veil of maya shall be removed' and so be it accorded unto every man - for The Father has Willed it so - and so be it ---

Are ye not one of His Chosen - that ye may receive of His fullness? - and that ye be brought into the place wherein He is? -

wherein ye shall have thy birthright given unto thee? -- And so be it that the way shall be shown thee and ye have but to walk therein - for all barriers shall be removed - and ye shall be as one set straight upon it -- And ye shall give unto thyself credit for thy own strength to walk with equilibrium and surety ---

Be ye alert and hear that which is said - and ye shall be rewarded in great measure -- And forget not it is but the beginning of thy new part - for it shall be given unto thee as ye are prepared to receive -- And so be it that there are many prepared to receive of The Father - Son and Holy Ghost ---

And blest are they which are so prepared - for they shall receive their inheritance -- And be ye at peace and know from whence ye come - and for that ye shall receive of Him which shall come unto thee - and ye shall be quickened of Him and ye shall be as one come alive - and ye shall have great joy - and peace shall abide within thee -- So be it unto thee in The Name of The Most High ---

I Am thy Older Brother - The Poseid - The Brotherhood of The Emerald Cross ---- Recorded by Sister Thedra of The Brotherhood of The Emerald Cross ---

Brother Bor

Beloved Ones which receive of My Words - and which receive of My strength and Love: I am come into the world of men for the purpose of giving thee courage to meet the future events which are soon to take place upon the Earth -- Ye have been told of that over and over again - yet ye have given no credence unto it ---

89

And I stand be and give it unto thee as it is given unto Me of The Father to say unto thee - "That they know whereof they speak" -- And it will serve thee well to listen - for it is the way of the black dragon to beguile thee -- As ye are within the place where he is - and where he has his being - ye are in his den - and he is not of a mind to loose thee ---

Are ye not mindful of Them which would deliver thee out of his den? Wherein have ye been told that he shall be bound? - ye are as one hypnotized by him - and ye shall be delivered! Will it so! - and ye shall have thy freedom -- Many which have worked for eons of time for the freedom of all men are now coming into the Earth to assist - for <u>man</u> <u>and</u> <u>Earth</u> <u>shall</u> <u>be</u> <u>freed</u> - and they shall know no more darkness -- Would that I could be unto thee thy deliverance - yet ye have but to say the Word -- Ye have that power within thyself and it shall be unto thee thy passport ---

For as ye will it - so be it unto thee - was it not so from the beginning? For as ye asked for thy present condition was it given unto thee -- Ye are thy own 'pointer' and ye point thyself thy own place -- And it is given unto Me to remind thee - as ye have forgotten thy oneness with thy Source -- So be it ye shall remember - and return of thy own will! Blest are they which seek their Source for they shall find It and they shall be glad -- Be ye of a mind to receive that which shall be revealed unto them which seek ---

For much revelation is to be given thru many sources - and it shall profit thee to be prepared to receive of The Father - Son and Holy Ghost -- And so be it given unto thee according to thy will - and in The Name of The Most High ---

90

I Am thy Older Brother - Bor - of The Order of The Emerald Cross --- Recorded by Sister Thedra - Order of The Emerald Cross

Part #17

Blest of my Being: Now it shall be given unto thee a part for 'them' which shall be sent to them whose duty is to get it to 'them' which await the Words of The Mother Sara - for She has prepared a Part for 'them' and they shall profit thereby - and so be it and Beleis ---

Mother Sara

Blest of My Being: I come unto thee with the Part which has been prepared for 'them' which are to receive the Words of Our Blessed Mother Sara -- And She has given it unto them with the blessing of The Father and The Mother -- And so be it that it shall bless them in The Name of The Father - Son and Holy Ghost - Amen -- And so be it and Beleis ---

Blest of My Presence - ye the children of My Heart - which I hold so dear - and so near -- I am thy Mother Sara - from Whom ye have gone out - and to Whom ye shall return - and there shall be great joy - and much gladness - for long have We awaited thy return -- I am prepared to receive thee - and I am prepared to be unto thee all that ye shall need - for I have kept for thee thy inheritance - and ye shall be given it in its entirety -- And ye shall know no want for it is a bountiful inheritance ---

And ye shall be as the wanderer no more - for ye have finished thy sojourn within the places of darkness - and ye shall walk in the Light which never fails -- And ye shall know thy Source and ye shall not separate thyself again -- Now it is told thee that ye shall be brought into the place of The Most High - and so be it that ye shall - and therein is Mercy and Wisdom - for ye know not that which ye have separated thyself from -- And be it given unto thee to remember - and for that have I made Myself known unto thee - that ye shall remember Me and the place from which ye went out ---

And so be it that ye shall awaken unto the Light which burns upon thy own altar and within the Inner Temple ---

And many are prepared to receive thee within the place wherein I am ---

And so be it that there shall be many come unto thee that ye may be prepared (PPP) to enter into the place wherein I am -- I have kept thy place - and I shall be glad to receive thee -- And so be it - Selah ---

Sara thy Mother - and the fortune of The Father and which holds thee within the Light of the Christ - and so be it that ye shall walk therein forever more - and Selah ---

Sara - Order of The Emerald Cross ---

Recorded by Sister Thedra - Order of The Emerald Cross ---

Blest of My Being: Be ye now prepared to receive that which has been prepared for 'them' by thy Brother Gabriel - for He has given unto them a new Part - and it shall profit them ---

And ye shall be His hand made manifest unto them - and so be it that ye shall be blest of Him - and of the Father - Son and Holy Ghost - Amen ---

Gabriel

Beloved of Earth - and the children of Light: Was it not on the Star Ship that ye said: "I shall remember thee - and I shall return?" - and have ye not forgotten thy promise - and have ye not been away a long time? I am at the helm of the Star Ship - and I am prepared to bring Her nigh unto the Earth - where I shall receive many which have the fortune to be brought within the port wherein I shall await them ---

Ye have not prepared thyself for this day! Yet it is come that I shall be upon the horizon whereon I shall wait -- And when the hour strikes I shall put into port and I shall receive them which are prepared to enter the Star Ship -- Ye shall remember that which ye have said - and thy Covenant with Me - and ye shall be prepared for that which shall be revealed of thy Portion which shall be given unto thee - and ye shall be glad for knowing! It is given unto Me to keep watch and to guard the coast of thy Earth - and therein is wisdom - for it is portioned unto Her to be passing thru shallow waters where are rugged shoals - and wherein is much danger -- I am one of many which are responsible for Her safety ---

And so be it that I shall keep guard until She has safely reached Her new berth -- And it is with great responsibility which has been given unto Us of The Father that She shall be brought safely into Her berth wherein She shall rest - and wherein She shall receive them which are prepared to share Her <u>new joy</u> and <u>freedom</u> -- Be ye blest of My Presence - and I shall stand ready to receive thee -- And so be it done in The Name of The Father - Son and Holy Ghost - Amen - Selah --

I am thy Servant and thy Older Brother in the service of The Christ which ye shall come to know --- Gabriel - Brotherhood of The 7 Rays ---

Recorded by Sister Thedra - School of 7 Rays --

Part #18

Blest of My Being: Will it not profit 'them' to receive of the One and only Beautealu - and His Father The Poseid? I have given unto thee the Portions which they have prepared for 'them' and now ye shall give unto them another -- For it is but the beginning of Their revelations unto them ---

And so shall it profit them much -- And it is given unto thee to be their hands made manifest - so they may receive that which is of The Father - Son and Holy Ghost -- So be it and Beleis--

Beautealu

Blest of Earth - and the children of the land (America): Wherein have ye given credit for that which has been given unto thee by The Father of Us - which has given unto Us Life - and provided that which is necessary unto it? ---

Was it not given unto man to inherit the Earth and the fullness thereof? ---

And now I say unto thee - he shall! But ye have to be prepared for that which ye have inherited -- For ye have been in no wise prepared for that -- As it has been given unto thee to forget thy birthright - ye have sold it for a poor penny -- And now ye shall purchase it back at a great cost! - for it is a pity that ye have been so nearsighted that ye did not see that which was in store for thee -- I have given of Myself that ye might have thy eyes opened - and that ye might remember thy Father and Mother from which ye went out -- Are ye not reminded of Them every day - when ye behold thyself

96

which was made in Their likeness and wherein has thy Life been sustained? And were it not for Their <u>Love</u> and <u>Mercy</u> ye would have destroyed thyself - and for that have They remembered thee ---

And They have opened the doors that ye may return unto Them ---

As it were in the days of the Lotus ye have remembered Them not - and ye shall be reminded of Them again and again! Blest are they which are reminded - for they shall be made to remember their Source - and they shall be brought back -- <u>Will</u> it <u>so</u>! And so shall it be ---

I am in the place wherein are many which have gone the Royal Road - and they have said that it shall be given unto thee to enter this route -- And ye shall know that which is given unto every man of The Father - that which was given unto Our Brother Sananda (Jesus) to know when He conquered death -- He has given of Himself that ye may know the same freedom ---

Yet ye have not comprehended that which He gave unto thee!

Now it is given unto Him to walk among thee - and ye have not awakened unto his presence -- He has given His Word that He should return - and so He has! And ye have not asked audience with Him -- Ye shall come to know many which are thy Elders on the Way of the Royal Road -- And ye shall be given the mind to listen to that which They say -- Be ye as a little child and fortune thyself that which thy Father has for thee -- Ye have profited little from that which ye have gathered from books - it has been unto thee a barrier

- for ye have been blinded by <u>men's</u> <u>opinions</u> and the experiences of others ---

Will ye not begin thy own search for Truth - and listen unto the Voice which shall be heard throughout the land? and which shall be unto thee thy <u>own</u> <u>deliverance</u>! Be ye prepared - for many shall come unto thee - and They shall give thee courage and strength for that which ye shall encounter ---

As it is given unto Me and My Father to prepare thee for the place which shall be prepared for thee - ye shall have much given unto thee by Us which have come to <u>sibor</u> thee - and to heal thy blindness and thy <u>amnesia</u> - for ye have indeed lost thy memory -- So shall ye be healed within thy parts which are of the Earth - and ye shall step forth in thy glorified body made new -- And so be it and Selah --- I am thy Older Brother Beautealu - which has come unto thee by the Grace and Mercy of Our Father in Whose Name I am come unto all who are prepared to receive Me -- Selah ---

Blest of my Being: Will it not profit 'them' to receive of the Posied - the Father of Beautealu - and that which He has prepared for them -- So be it that they shall be prepared to receive in greater measure - and so be it and Beleis ---

The Posied

Blest of My Presence - and of the Father which has sent Me unto thee -- For it is come that I shall reveal Myself unto them which are prepared to receive Me -- I shall give unto thee of My knowledge and of My strength - and courage ---

I shall give unto thee that which shall be unto thee meat - and unto thee wine which shall not intoxicate thee -- It shall be unto thee the Elixir of Life and ye shall be as ye are known unto Us - not as ye appear unto thyself -- For ye see only that which is thy 'Earthly port' - and not the 'flame which burns within' - therein is thy oneness with all men - and with The Father ---

Fortune thyself that which shall be revealed unto thee - for I stand ready to open the flood gates - that all may be revealed unto them which are prepared to receive that which has been kept secret -- And all that which has been hidden from the unjust and the imprudent ---

Were it not wise to say these things unto thee I should not say them! The time is come when ye shall have thy head unbound - and ye shall know thyself as ye are known unto Us thy Older Brothers - which see beyond thy port (Earthly garment) and ye shall know wherein ye are staid -- Be ye at one with Me - and ye shall have thy eyes opened - and they shall behold all things made new -- And for that have We come unto thee - that ye may be made ready for great revelation which shall be given unto 'them' which are ready to receive of The Father - Son and Holy Ghost -- I am within the secret place. (ΔΔΔ) wherein I am to receive.

Part #19

Blest of My Being: Will it not profit 'them' to receive of the One and only Solomena - and that which She has prepared for them? For it is given unto her to be the "Goddess of Wisdom" -- And She has much which She has kept for them for this time - and it shall be given unto them as they are prepared to receive it -- And so be it and Beleis ---

Solomena

Blest of My Being - and the children of Earth: Will ye not partake of My Love - and of My Knowledge ---

I have been within the place wherein all things are known - and I have been prepared to give unto thee that ye may be prepared for a New Age - that ye might come into thy fullness - and that ye may receive that which has been kept for thee -- In no wise shall ye forget thy own fortune - for ye shall be given that which has been kept for thee ---

And it has been planned that ye shall become of age - and that ye shall be told that which has been kept secret -- And so be ye prepared for the great learning - and a great speaking - and a great gathering in -- And so shall it be - and ye shall be prepared for that which shall be given unto thee to say ---

For ye shall be the Mouth of The Father made manifest - and ye shall say that which He puts into thy mouth to say - and ye shall do that which he gives unto thee to do ---

And ye shall know that which ye say - and so is given unto thee by The Father and ye shall be glad to be His Servant -- And so be ye prepared for that which shall be fortuned unto thee of The Father - and so be it in His Name - and of The Son and Holy Ghost -- Amen and Selah ---

Solomena - Brotherhood of The Emerald Cross --- Recorded by Sister Thedra - Brotherhood of The Emerald Cross -

Blest of My Being: Will it not profit 'them' to receive of The One and only Posied - and that which He has prepared for them -- He has given them much - and He has much that shall be given unto them - and it shall profit them -- So be it given in The Name of The Father - Son and Holy Ghost -- Amen ---

The Posied

Beloved Ones of Earth: Be ye blest of My Being and of My Presence - for I am come that ye may receive Me and that which I bring unto thee -- I am with thee that ye might come to know thyself and thy Oneness with all mankind - and that ye may come to know thy Source - and that ye may return unto It and be made Whole -- Ye have been told and told - that ye are One with The Father - yet ye have not comprehended the fullness of thy fortune - for it is given unto thee to be fashioned in His Likeness - and He has given unto thee all that He Is - and all that He has ---

And ye grovel within the swine's burrow - and ye have fasted upon feast days - and ye have repeated thy prayers as 'rigmaroles' which are operated as by a coin machine -- Ye have not given of thyself unto Him -- Ye have said that which has been prompted by

101

darkness - and ye have not been given to say that which should lift up thy brother ---

Nor have ye been unto thy own self true -- Ye have given of thyself and of thy energy unto the forces of darkness - and yet ye profess to be a disciple of The Christ which ye comprehend not -- Ye have been in no wise acceptable unto the Light of The Christ ---

For wherein there is Light there is no darkness - and ye have served the forces of darkness - ye have fed the 'black dragon' - he has fattened on thy food - and he has been unto thee a god which ye have served with all thy strength! And now it is come that the black dragon shall die of hunger! - for ye shall feed him no more! - for ye shall learn that he is thy enemy and the cause of thy sorrow and thy torment -- Ye shall turn from him - and ye shall seek deliverance from him - and ye shall be delivered - for there are many sent into the Earth for the purpose of delivering thee ---

And so be ye prepared for that which shall be given unto thee -- And it shall profit thee to be prepared - for the time is come when thy head shall be unbound - and ye shall see and ye shall know that which has bound thee - and ye shall know wherein is thy freedom - So be it given unto thee that which is thy salvation and thy deliverance from bondage -- And so be it that ye be prepared to receive Them which shall come unto thee with that which would loose thee - and be unto thee Light wherein ye shall be loosed -- And so be it accorded unto thee as ye would have it - and Selah ---

I am thy Older Brother The Posied of The Brotherhood of The Emerald Cross --- Recorded by Sister Thedra --

Blest of My Being: Will it not profit them to receive of The Blessed Mother Sara - and that which She has prepared for them - and that which shall be given in The Name of The Father - Son and Holy Ghost -- So be it that it shall profit them - and Beleis ---

Blessed Mother Sara

Beloved Children - whom I hold so dear - and so close: Will ye not remember Me and return unto Me? It has been given unto Me to hold thee fast - and to keep thee within My Bosom - while ye have forgotten Me and thy fortune which ye have denounced -- And will ye not return to claim it? For in no wise has it been spent - it awaits thy return and ye have but to claim it ---

I am come unto thee that ye may remember - and that ye may return unto Me -- as it not given unto thee to go into the world of darkness for thy own satisfaction? - wherein ye became drugged on the fermentation of the new wine - and ye became intoxicated with the liquor of the new saloons - and ye forgot the Bread of Life and the Elixir which has the power to give Life -- Ye have staggered wherein ye should walk with equilibrium ---

And ye have not know of the ones which have held thee within the palm of Their hands that ye may reach the age of account ability - and that ye may not destroy thyself – Ye have not given credit unto Them for Their Love and Protection -- Now that ye have been reminded again and again of Them which have guarded thee - will it not suffice thee? And will ye not bestir thyself and come into the place which has been kept for thee? I am thy Mother Sara - Who has awaited thy return - and which shall receive thee with great joy - in

The Name of The Father - Son and Holy Ghost - Selah -- Brotherhood of The Emerald Cross ---

Recorded by Sister Thedra ---

Beloved of My Being: - And now ye shall have that which is prepared for 'them' by The One and only Gabriel which has given unto them of His Love and Protection - that they might be spared for this day -- And so be it given unto them in The Name of The Father - Son and Holy Ghost - Amen and Beleis ---

Gabriel

Blest Children of Earth: I am thy Servant and thy Older Brother Gabriel -- Would that ye could see as We which have a greater vision see - and that ye could have the wisdom of Solomena - and the power of The Posied - and there would be no need of My giving ye this portion ---

Yet it is not time to put up My Armor and go home -- For there is much to be accomplished before we can give unto Ourself the Portion which has been kept for Us -- Wherein is it said that We too serve The Christ -- So be it -- And not until the last vestige of darkness is dispelled from the Earth shall We partake of Our Portion -- For it has been given unto Us to keep watch - and We sleep not! neither do we give unto Ourself that which would be unto Ourself that which would be unto Us a sedative ---

For We are vigilant and true to Our trust and unto Ourself -- As ye have been within the places wherein ye have given credit unto thyself for all that ye have accomplished within the Earth - wherein

104

have ye been able to read the records of the Heavens - and the records of the Akasia? And on what star is thy name written? And whereupon have ye given unto them which have given unto thee all that ye have credit? ---

Ye have nothing! Ye have nothing! Not the air that ye breathe belongs to thee -- Ye are but puppets within the hands of The Father -- And wherein is it said: "Ye shall return unto Him?" - and then ye shall come into thy own - for it is from Him and by Him that ye have thy being ---

And from Him ye have gone out - and to Him ye shall return - and so be it in The Name of The Most High ---

And be ye prepared to enter into the place of The Most High ---

I am thy Older Brother and thy Servant in the Light of The Christ --- Gabriel - of The Emerald Cross ---

Recorded by Sister Thedra ---

Part #20

Blest of My Being: Will it not profit 'them' to partake of the wisdom of Solomena -- And will it not profit them to hear that which She says unto 'them' ---

And so be it that She has prepared a new part for them and it shall be given unto them in The Name of The Father - Son and Holy Ghost -- Amen and Beleis ---

Solomena

Blest of my Being: I am come unto thee that ye may receive that which has been kept for thee for this day -- And it is given unto Me to know whereof I speak - for it is My fortune to be within the place wherein all things are known -- And I shall be prepared to receive unto Myself them which are prepared to enter into the place wherein I am -- And it will profit thee to hear that which I say unto thee - for in the time which is near - it shall be accorded unto thee to be in the place wherein ye are purchased - and ye shall be as one with no place to lay thy head ---

And ye shall be as one which has given unto the 'pore' all thy substance -- And wherein has it been said – 'that the pore shall be returned unto the Elements - and ye shall stand forth in thy glorified body made new?' And so be it and give unto that which is Eternal that which shall profit thee! ---

For it is said that "there shall be a great awakening and a great gathering in" - and so be it and Beleis ---

And ye shall be in the place wherein ye are prepared - for the day draweth nigh when ye shall remember the days of thy wanton - and ye shall remember these Words of warning - for I have said them before - and ye have not comprehended ---

And so be it that ye shall learn the hard way - for it is given unto thee to be within the place wherein shall be many changes - and many new experiences shall beset thee -- And ye shall be wise indeed to give unto Me credit for telling thee what is before thee - for to be forewarned is to be forearmed - and ye shall be fortuned that which ye fortune unto thyself ---

For it is given unto many to say that which I have said - and ye have not given credence unto them -- Before thee are the signs and the part which has been given unto thee shall indicate that which is to follow -- Be ye wise as a fox and ye shall find a place wherein to burrow - and in no wise shall ye be destroyed! yet ye may suffer much torment! ---

Would that I could pick thee up as a straw and deliver thee - yet it is not lawful - for ye shall be prepared (PPP) for thy deliverance - and ye shall not be without guidance - for We which are of the Losoloes know wherein ye are and wherein ye are prepared ---

And We have called unto thee as one would call unto a ship which is running onto an island of coral - and wherein have ye been warned - again and again? Be ye blest of My Portion unto thee and of My Presence - and I shall come unto thee again - and again that ye may be alert - and comprehend that which ye have been given -- So be it and Selah -- I am thy Servant in The Name of The Most High - and so be it that ye shall have thy head unbound and ye shall

107

have that which has been kept for thee -- Solomena - Order of The Emerald Cross -- Recorded by Sister Thedra - Order of The Emerald Cross

Blest of my Being: Now it shall be given unto thee to receive that which is prepared for 'them' by the One and only Michael - which has given them so much - and was He not prepared for His Part - and was I not prepared for Mine? ---

So be it given unto them that they too may be prepared for a new part and so be it that it shall profit them -- So be it and Beleis ---

Michael

Beloved who are My sheep - and who are the ones I hold within My heart: I am the One which is given to preachments - and I am the One which carries the 'Flaming Sword' - and so shall ye be reminded of Me when ye are given chastisement - for it is My part to keep thee in green pastures and near fresh waters ---

And I come unto thee at this time as never before - that ye may heed the Shepherd's call - and that ye may hear that which He says -- For in the time which is near thy pasture shall be dried up - and the waters shall no longer be sweet ---

And ye shall be put into a new place wherein the waters shall be cool and refreshing ---

And now ye shall be unto thyself true - and ye shall give unto them audience - for I am come unto thee in The Name of The Father Which has sent Me and I ask of thee - heed My Words - for they shall be unto thee that which shall suffice thee - and ye shall know that which I have said unto thee in this parable to be true -- For ye shall stand upon the Earth a testimony of My Words unto thee - and ye shall remember them ---

It is given unto Me to say that which is given unto Me by The Father - and in no wise does He deceive Me -- Wherein has it been said that great changes shall come upon the Earth - and so be it! and ye shall not have thy comforts which ye know - and ye shall be within thy beds - within thy places of laughter - within thy temples - and within thy places of entertainment - when ye shall be brought out! - and ye shall say: Lord! Lord! where art Thou? ---

I give unto thee that which should profit thee - and it shall be unto thee that which ye would have it -- And ye shall be within the place wherein ye are prepared for that which shall come upon thee and upon the Earth ---

I am thy Shepherd and Servant of The Christ - Michael - School of 7 Rays -- Recorded by Sister Thedra - School of 7 Rays

Blest of My Being: Ye shall now receive that which is prepared for thee by the One and only Osiris - for He has given unto 'them' a new part and it shall profit them much -- And so be it given unto them in The Name of The Father - Son and Holy Ghost - Amen and Beleis ---

Osiris

Blest of Earth: Be ye blest of My Being - and of The Father Which has sent Me unto thee -- I am come in His Name and in His Service that ye may know Him and thy oneness with Him -- Are ye not mindful of Him and that which He has given unto thee? Wherein have ye profited by giving thought of thy pore? And wherein have ye profited by thy own pore? ---

It is given unto thee to be always the Light which burns within the pore -- The pore is the instrument of the Flame - and the Flame has many instruments ---

Yet ye are in no wise one of the instruments - for the Flame knows no bound -- Yet in the night time of thy travails ye have dreamed ye are bound -- And ye have been 'given unto thinking' and ye have thought thyself to be ensouled in the pore - and ye have given unto it the power to dictate unto thee - to give unto thee that which ye call pain or pleasure -- And ye have given unto it credit for being the 'great self' -- And wherein is it said that the "I Am" shall not have any bond or bondage? As ye have given unto thyself credit for all thy fortune - ye have gathered thistles wherein there is wheat - and wherein is much grain of much nourishment ---

As ye have sown unto the pore ye have sown tares - and ye have been poor in nourishment -- For it is given unto thee to reap as ye have sown ---

And now the day of harvest is come - and ye stand as one hungered and as one lean from thy hunger ---

And be ye as one which has learned from thy folly - for now ye shall sow again - and many bring thee seeds of a new grain which ye shall receive in abundance -- And ye shall nourish them - and they shall grow and multiply - and they shall be unto thee as one thousand times that of the old -- And ye shall be glad that ye have

accepted that which has been given in Love - Mercy and Wisdom -
--

I am thy Older Brother of The Inner Temple of Osiris - in the Service of The Most High - Which ye shall come to know -- And so be it - Selah ---

Recorded by Sister Thedra - School of 7 Rays --

Part #21

Blest of My Being: Will it not profit 'them' to have that Which is prepared for them by Our Brother and by The Father - which shall be unto them much wisdom -- It is now given unto thee to receive that which is prepared for them by the One and only Beautealu ---

Beautealu

Blest of My Presence: Ye shall be unto Me My sibets - for I am sent unto thee as Sibor -- And ye shall be as the one in a school room - for is it not given unto thee to be in school? And it shall be as a farther advanced one - for now re are coming of age - and ye shall enter the school of the Losoloes wherein ye shall be taught that which shall profit thee -- And wherein ye shall be taught the laws of the Omniverse - and wherein ye shall learn to control that which is given into thy keeping - and wherein ye shall learn that which is of the Eternal Verities -- And be ye so prepared that ye may be acceptable unto thy Sibors - for not all are acceptable - only them which are prepared -- For there are places for them which are not prepared for the Losolo ---

And will ye not give of thy energy that ye may enter into the place wherein all things are known ---

And for this have We thy Sibors been sent unto thee -- And so may ye give us thy attention and thy respect - for We represent thee before the throne of The Father - and We bring unto thee that which He gives unto Us for thee -- And will ye not be prepared to receive it - for He has much which He has kept for thee -- And now it is given unto some in part - and yet the whole awaits thee -- And be ye not deceived for The Father knoweth wherein ye are prepared and wherein ye are lacking -- And give unto Him credit for thy being and give unto Him thy will and thy energy and thy thanks! - and He shall pass thee into the higher places wherein ye shall be prepared to enter into the place wherein He is - and therein ye shall receive without limit - for He has willed it so - and so be it and Selah -- I am thy Brother and Sibor Beautealu - and thy Servant in the Light of the Christ - which ye shall come to know - and so be unto thee as ye would have it -- Selah ---

Blest of My Being: Ye shall now be prepared for a new part which shall be given unto thee by the One and only Posied -- And it shall be given unto thee in the Name of The Father - Son and Holy Ghost - so be it and Beleis ---

The Posied

Blest of My Presence and of My Being: I am comes that ye may be at one with Me and with The Father - for We are One - and ye too shall become one with Him ---

Wherein is it said: "Come unto Me and be ye made whole"? - for ye have gone out from Him in parts - and ye shall gather up thyself and return unto Him - wherein ye shall be at one with Him - -

As it is given unto Me to see wherein ye are staid - I can say - ye are one with Him - ye comprehend it not ---

And ye shall come to know thyself - and thy oneness with all men -- And ye shall have that which was meant for thee from the beginning - Ye have squandered thy portion which has been given unto thee -- And now the day of reckoning has come - and ye shall be as one which has given unto the wolves that which was meant for thee and for thy children - and ye shall have them at thy door -- Ye shall be given the strength and wisdom to slay them - for they are in no wise thy master ---

Are ye not of a mind to be in thy place - prepared to receive that which is given unto thee as thy inheritance of The Father -- And will it not be unto thee thy deliverance from that which is thy bondage -- I am prepared to give unto thee all that ye are capable fo receiving - for ye shall be made ready for that which shall be unto thee a portion which shall be unto thee both 'bitter' and 'sweet' ---

And we thy Sibors stand in the high places and We see that which is before thee - and that which ye shall encounter -- And be ye at peace and know that We are with thee - and We shall know Our Own - and We shall come unto thee that ye shall be delivered up -- And again I say unto thee: "Be at peace" and give The Father thanks for thy being - and He shall deliver thee out of darkness - for He has willed it so - And so be it and Selah and Beleis -- I am thy Older Brother and thy Servant in the Light of the Christ - The Posied - Brotherhood of The Emerald Cross ---

Recorded by Sister Thedra - Brotherhood of The Emerald Cross –

Blest of My Being: Will it not profit 'them' to receive that which has been prepared for them by the One and only Beautealu - and so be it that it shall profit them -- And be it given unto them in the Name of The Father - Son and Holy Ghost - Amen and Beleis---

114

Beautealu

Blest of My Being: I am thy Older Brother which has been sent unto thee of The Father that ye might have the Portion which I am to give unto thee -- One which We know as Sananda Jesus) has asked The Father that I come out of the place wherein I have been that I might add My Light unto His -- For it is a time of great activity within the Earth - and many hands have reached out that The Father's Plans might be fulfilled -- And when it is given unto one of Us to be called We come with great haste - for We are given to obedience - and wherein is it said that "There shall be obedience unto the call"! And so be it ---

And it shall be given unto many to hear the call - for it has gone out thru the Cosmos -- Be ye blest that ye may hear it - and have the wisdom to answer it! Be ye as one which listens that ye may hear it and know it! As it shall be given unto thee according to thy will -- And will it so! And so shall it be unto thee - The Father has given His Word that all shall hear His Voice and know it -- And so be it and Selah -- Before thee is a Plan which has been given unto ye children of Earth - and ye shall have great revelation concerning it -- And for this has many revealed themselves as Sibors of the New Age ---

And it is given unto Me to be one of them -- I have been unto thee Sibor many times - and ye have not remembered Me -- I am One of Them which have been within the land of the Lotus - and wherein I gave of My time and energy unto The Father's Work -- And ye have been in the places wherein I have sibored -- Some have been fortuned to remember - some have forgotten - some have gone the "Royal Road" -- And yet We come again to the time of gathering in - and there shall be great gathering together and there shall be great joy and much gladness -- And for that have I come that ye may remember thy day within the Temples of the Lotus and within the places which ye have long forgotten --

And ye shall remember The Father and thy part with Him - and so be it as ye will it -- And be ye as one which knows wherein ye are staid and so be it unto thee -- Blest are they which ask of The Father for they shall receive of Him ---

I am thy Older Brother Beautealu - Son of the Posied - and Servant of The Most High -- Brotherhood of the Seven Rays ---

Recorded by Sister Thedra - Brotherhood of the Seven Rays -

The Posied

Blest of My Presence: I am the Posied - Father of Beautealu-- I too have answered the call -- It is given unto them of the Inner Temple to have the fortune of The Father - and We are given to obedience - - And it is a part of wisdom that one listens with respect and devotion unto the Sibor -- We which have been within the Temples wherein We have given of Ourself - know the shortcomings - and too We know the devotion of the sibet unto his Sibors - for it is given to the devoted one to receive that which is portioned out unto him -- His time and his energy is not divided - and he stands upon the precepts of The Father and upon the Portions which is given unto him - he falters not - and he keeps his own council - and therein is wisdom! - --

116

Blest is the one which keeps his council! for he shall receive of his own account and he shall be rewarded abundantly ---

As it is given unto Me to be One with The Father - and as I know His will - and as I do His will - I am within the place wherein ye shall go which are prepared to go into the Secret Place wherein all things are known - And forget not this is the day of preparation - for it is given unto the Earth and man to be prepared for a new place -- And so be it and Selah -- This is My Portion unto thee -- I shall come again and again - and so be it that ye shall remember Me ---

I am thy Older Brother and Servant of The Most High - The Posied - of The Order of The Emerald Cross ---

Blest of My Being: Now ye shall receive that which is prepared for 'them' by thy Brother and Sibor - the One and only Michael - for He has prepared a new part for them - and so be it given in the Name of The Father - Son and Holy Ghost - Amen and Beleis -

Michael

Blest of Earth - and them which are My sheep: I am come unto thee that ye may have more food - and of greater strength -- I am in the place wherein the pasture is green - and wherein the waters are sweet -- I am prepared to receive thee - for the pasture wherein I am is 'new' and the fertile valleys and rolling hills beckon unto thee ---

Within this place are many shepherds and they know their flock - and they have been prepared to move them to higher ground wherein is an abundance of everything which ye shall need ---

I am in the place wherein I shall receive My Own - and they shall not want - for it is given unto Me to provide for My Own and therein is The Father's will -- And so be it that ye too shall do the will of The Father - for He has kept thee for this day -- And so shall it be that ye shall come to know Him -- And be ye at one with Him and ye shall return unto Him - and He shall receive thee in love and mercy ---

Be ye prepared for that which shall be fortuned unto thee of The Father - for He has kept a Portion for thee which shall be given unto thee within the time which is near -- And be it such as shall profit thee - and so be it and Selah ---

I am thy Shepherd and Sibor and Servant of The Father in the Light of the Christ which ye shall come to know - Michael - School of the 7 Rays ---

Recorded by Sister Thedra - School of the 7 Rays --

Lake Titicaca - Peru-Bolivia –

Part #22

Blest of My Being: Will it not profit 'them' to receive that which has been given unto them of The Father - and shall they not receive of Him of their own account? And so be it and Baleis ---

The Father

Blest My Children - which have gone out from Me - and which shall return unto Me:

I am in the place wherein I shall receive My Own - and ye shall return unto Me perfect - even as ye went out ---

And ye shall be in the place wherein ye are prepared for thy return -- I have sent many unto thee that ye may be prepared! - for I am of a mind to bring thee home -- I have given unto thee a new dispensation wherein ye may hasten thy coming -- And I have been unto thee both food and drink - for ye have hungered in a land of plenty ---

I am come unto thee that ye may be prepared for thy new part - and for thy new place or abode -- And ye shall receive them which I have sent unto thee in My Name - and in the Light of the Christ - for it has not been revealed unto them that which it is - for ye have not prepared thyself to receive of this part which has been kept for thee ---

Ye shall come to know that which is the Christ - for ye shall be prepared for it - and ye shall not return into darkness again - for I have decreed that ye shall be brought out of darkness -- And ye shall have thy being in the Light of Christ - and ye shall be as I am - and equal unto Me - for We have Our Being within the Light which never fails --

As ye ask so be it unto thee for I have sent Many unto thee that ye shall remember thy being - and return unto thy Source - so be it that ye shall be delivered out of thy bondage ---

And I am within the place wherein I am prepared to receive thee -- And so be it that ye shall know the Christ - and walk within the Light which is Eternal - and Selah ---

I am thy Father - The One which has sent thee out - and which shall bring thee back ---

Blest of My Being: Will it not profit 'them' to receive that which is prepared for them by the One and only Solomena –

And so be it given unto them in the Name of The Father - Son and Holy Ghost - Amen and Beleis ---

Solomena

Blest of My Being: I am come unto thee that ye shall have more Light and wisdom -- Be ye of a mind to receive that which has been given unto Me of The Father - for it shall be unto thee all things -- And ye shall be given according to thy capacity to receive ---

And it is My part to increase thy capacity for learning - for it is given unto Me to be within the place wherein all things are known - and wherein they which are prepared shall be brought -- And it is given unto Me to receive thee within the place wherein I am - and so be it as ye would have it - and Selah -- For the fortune of The Father shall be at thy disposal - and ye shall know such freedom and joy as ye have never known ---

Blest are they which enter into the place wherein I am - for they shall have the fortune which is their inheritance ---

I have been within the place wherein all things are known for a long time and I have received many - and they too shall be glad to receive thee ---

Come into this place and receive of Our wisdom - and Our Love - and our mercy - and ye shall not want nor suffer more - for I shall be unto thee all that ye shall need ---

Be ye prepared for that which I shall bring unto thee - for this is the beginning of My revelation unto thee - and as ye ask so shall ye receive -- And so be it as ye would have it ---

I am thy Sibor - and Servant in the Light of the Christ - and of The Most High - Solomena - of the Brotherhood of the Emerald Cross---

Blest of My Being: Will it not profit 'them' to receive of the One and only Beautealu - and that which He has prepared for them? And so shall it be given unto them - and so be it in the Name of The Father - Son and Holy Ghost - Amen ---

Beautealu

I am come unto thee that ye may receive of The Father - and His Portion unto thee -- It is given unto Me to be One of Them which are within the place wherein is The Father - and I represent thee before the throne of the Father -- I have given unto thee much which should be unto thee "meat" and ye should profit thereby -- And ye should be in your place prepared to receive the "greater part" - yet ye shall wait for the "greater part" for ye are as babies without teeth -- Yet ye are growing up! and as ye can consume that which is more potent I shall give it unto thee - and so shall ye receive as ye are capable of consuming ---

Was it not told thee that I have come out from the place wherein I was? I was with The Father - and He has been prepared for this day - for it is come that ye shall be brought out of bondage and ye shall be prepared to enter into the place wherein He is ---

For the veil of mystery shall be removed! - and every man shall come to know The Father - as We which have come unto thee as Sibors-- And ye shall see Him and talk with Him even as We -- And be ye as one which wills it so! for as ye will it - so be it unto thee - Ye shall be provided all the proof which is necessary unto thee - for it is planned that there shall be some from among thee to be taken into the place wherein The Father is - and they shall return unto thee as a "living witness" and they shall be as ones 'made new' and they shall stand forth a living testimony of The Father's mercy and wisdom and of His Will ---

And so be ye prepared to receive in abundance - for I am with thee that ye may receive -- And so be it in The Name of The Most High and in the Light of The Christ - which ye shall come to know - and so be it as ye would have it -- I am thy Servant and Older

Brother Beautealu - School of The Seven Rays --

Blest of My Being: Ye have been called in from the hill for a part which shall be given unto 'them' by the One and only Zamu - for it is now time that Ho reveal Himself unto 'them' which await more Light from the Inner Temple -- And ye shall be unto Him His hands made manifest in the world of men -- And it shall be given unto thee from The Father - Son and Holy Ghost - Amen and Beleis ---

Zamu

Blest of my Being: I am sent unto thee of The Father that ye may be alert - and that ye may be made to hear with thy inner ear - and that which I say unto thee shall serve to alert thee -- For it is given unto many to say the things which the Father has given unto them to say unto thee - and ye have not heard that which they have said!

Ye look but ye see not! Ye hear with thy outer ear - and it is but sound which ye comprehend not!

Now it is given unto Me to open thy inner ear and ye shall be given understanding and comprehension -- Ye are now entering the school or preparation and ye shall be as ones which has presented thyself for examination - for examined ye shall be! and each unto his own place -- For the day of separation is at hand -- And ye shall be given as ye have portioned unto thyself - for it is the law: "as ye sow so shall ye reap" -- And it shall behoove thee to accept the new seed which has been proffered thee - And We which are sent unto thee at this time are to prepare the ground for the "new seed"- We have been called the "plowmen of The Father" ---

So are We - for We have come unto thee to prepare tree for that which shall be given unto thee - and that which shall come upon thee - and upon the Earth ---

Each of us have our parts - for some give unto thee hearing - some unto thee sight - some memory ---

Ye have not comprehended the vastness of The Father's business and the greatness of Our ministry unto thee -- And ye have not given thought of <u>that</u> <u>which</u> <u>ye</u> <u>shall</u> <u>become</u>! for it is given unto men of Earth to become GODS! -- And <u>even</u> <u>this</u> cannot tell them that which ye shall become - for it is beyond thy present comprehension ---

Some have come into the Earth that ye may have greater comprehension - some greater wisdom - others have come to break all barriers And We each work as the hands of The Father made manifest ---

I shall give unto thee as ye are capable of receiving - and I shall come unto thee as ye ask My Presence and give Me credence and port - for therein is the law - that ye may ask to receive -- And ye have but to ask and I am with thee in The Name of The Father which has sent Me from the place wherein He is ---

And ye shall be made to hear His Voice - in the Name of The Most High has it been given unto Me - that I might give unto thee - - And so be it that it shall profit thee in the Light of The Christ which ye shall come to know - I am thy Older Brother Zamu - Order of The Emerald Cross ---

Recorded by Sister Thedra of The Order of The Emerald Cross—

124

Part #23

Blest of My Being: Ye shall now receive that which has been given unto them of the One and only Posied - for He has prepared a part for them - and it shall profit them - and so be it and Beleis---

The Posied

Blest of My Being: Be ye blest of My Presence - for I am come unto thee that ye may have a "greater part" which has been kept for thee for this day -- And now it is come that ye shall have a new place of abode and a new part -- It shall behoove thee to prepare thyself for it -- For in the time which is near at hand - ye shall be put into a new place and ye shall be as ones which have been given that which ye have allotted unto thyself - for as ye are prepared so shall ye ask - and when ye are ready ye shall receive the "greater Part" ---

And it shall be given unto Me to give the "greater part" unto thee -- For I am sent unto thee of The Father - that ye may be prepared for the "greater part" - and so be it that ye may receive that which has been kept for thee - And now ye shall know them which are sent out from The Father that ye may be brought in - and so be it that many are sent and ye shall receive them in The Name of The Father - Son and Holy Ghost - Amen -- Blest are they which receive the messengers of The Father - for He has given unto them that which He would have thee accept from Him -- They are but His hands and feet made manifest - And as ye portion out unto them so shall ye receive of The Father - for as ye ask ye receive - "as ye sow - so shall ye reap"---

125

And be ye as one which has received of the "new seed" and it shall profit thee -- And I stand ready to replenish thy supply and to give unto thee strength and nourishment which shall suffice thee –

Be ye at peace and poise - for therein is wisdom! And ye shall come to know wherein thy strength lies! And be ye as one which can comprehend the things which I say unto thee - for I shall come unto thee again and again ---

And I shall give the greater nourishment - as ye are capable of consuming ---

So be it given in The Name of The Most High -- I am thy Older Brother - The Posied - of The Emerald Cross ---

Beautealu

Blest of My Being: I am thy Brother Beautealu - and I am come as My Father has come of The Father - Which has sent Us unto the Earth - that She and Her children be prepared for a new part which shall be given unto them ---

And ye have not heard that which has been said unto thee! for ye have not stirred thyself and ye shall be found wanting! For the time is nigh upon thee - and ye shall be caught up short of thy course! And ye shall begin over again - and thy memory shall be blanked from thee - and ye shall not remember thy being - and ye shall carry thy burdens on thy back - and ye shall till the soil with thy bare hands -- And ye shall have no memory of thy present science nor of the past -- For it is the law that ye shall learn! And is it not wise to heed that which is said and that which shall profit thee? - And so be it that it shall be said in many ways - and many times that ye may comprehend and progress on thy appointed course -- And be ye blest of The Father - Son and Holy Ghost –

I am thy Older Brother - Son of the Posied - Beautealu - of The School of the 7 Rays ---

Blest of My Being: One has revealed Himself as the "Beloved of the Emerald Isle" - which is known as Marshea - and ye shall receive Him in The Name of The Father - Which has given unto Him the fortune of humor -- So be it and Beleis ---

Marshea

Blest of My Presence: I am come unto thee that ye may know Me -- I am He which has given thee thy sense of humor -- And many times has it served thee well! For it is given unto man to be as one which gives unto himself all the credit! for he knows little of them which endow them with the gifts of life! I have given unto thee that which has been a shield and buckler in times of stress -- I have given unto thee that which has been unto thee a great asset -- And when ye said - it is now time to put up my armor and go home - I have given thee strength to laugh at thy weakness and frailties - and the courage to begin again --

I have held thee fast while ye have wept tears of acid!

I give unto thee that which shall be given unto them which await My Words - for it is given unto Me of The Father - and I give it unto thee -- And ye shall give it unto them and so be it that is shall reach them which await it -- So be it and Beleis ---

We which are in the secret place of The Most High are in no wise sad - nor do We appear without Our "sorg" - for We Who are of the "Royal Assembly" have been in many places wherein there is sadness - and We are alert unto thy heartaches -- And We give of Ourself that ye may quickly forget them and turn to the brighter side which We present unto thee ---

And it is given unto Me to be the Guardian of the "Emerald Isle" - and Her people once knew Me well! and in present time they remember Me only in legend and song -- Yet I am the One which has been given the opportunity to hold Her within my bosom - and to keep Her steadfast ---

And again She shall be as one <u>gone</u> <u>under</u> - and She shall have Her initiation within the briny deep -- And again She shall seek Her place within the Sun - and She shall be as one refreshed and cleansed -- So be it and Beleis ---

I am on the planet which ye call Mars - and thereon are many places where We can see every place - every one - and everything that exists upon the Earth ---

It is beyond thy comprehension! Yet the World - the Earth - is Our baby - And it shall grow up - grow to maturity - and We shall be glad! - for She has been a wayward child and She has been found wanting! There are many sent to Her that She may have as much help as We dare give Her - for it is not lawful to be unto Her all that We could be - for She shall be unto Herself a fortune lost - a fortune found -- And there shall be great joy thruout The Father's kingdom ---

So be it that We are sending One which shall stand with Her thru Her initiation and trial -- I am one which shall stand by and give of My strength and My Love -- And forget not that I am One which has gone the long way to bless thee - and to be unto thee that which ye shall come to know as an asset which is given unto thee of The Father: a sense of humor - for within it ye shall find strength and wisdom ---

So shall ye look up and see the face of One which has given unto thee warmth and sustained thee thru thy sojourn whithin the Earth -- And ye shall learn much and ye shall be given much which ye hitherto have not known - And so be it that The Father which has given Me passport unto thee - shall be unto thee all things and ye shall be free forevermore ---

I am thy Brother - thy Sibor of The Seven Rays - Marshea ---

Blest of My Being: Ye are on the whole blest of our Brother Marshea - and He has brot out of the silence that which shall be remembered! And ye shall give it unto them which shall be caused to remember Him -- And He has gone the long way to bless them ---

And now it shall be given unto many to stand within the place wherein He is - and He shall be prepared to receive them - And so be it and Beleis -- Sananda ---

Recorded by Sister Thedra of The School of Seven Rays --

129

Part #24

Blest of My Being: Ye shall now receive that which has been prepared for thee by the One which has revealed Himself unto thee - and which ye know as Coro - One which has been responsible for some of the Earth's records - and which have been hidden from the unjust and imprudent -- So be ye blest of His Presence and that which shall be given unto thee - which shall be given unto them which are prepared to receive that which He is prepared to give unto them -- So be it given in The Name of The Father - Son and Holy Ghost - Amen

Coro

Beloved - which shall be My hands made manifest unto them which are to receive of that which I am prepared to reveal unto them -- And will it not stand then <u>foursquare</u> to hear Me and that which I say unto them? ---

Now it is come that they which are prepared shall be given much which has hitherto been held in trust for them until they have reached the age of accountability -- And now it is come that there are a few which shall be given that which has been kept for them -- And so be it given unto them in The Name of The Father which has sent Me unto thee that this may be accomplished ---

And now it is My part to prepare them which have reached the age of accountability for that which shall be revealed unto them

They shall be taken into the place wherein the records of the Earth has been kept from Her beginning to the present time And it shall be a great revelation! For in no wise can the uninitiated comprehend the vastness of the part which She has played in The Father's plan - which shall be revealed unto them which are brot into the place of revelation ---

And now ye shall give ear unto Me - for I am come unto thee in love and wisdom - that ye may comprehend that which is given unto Me to give unto thee -- It is indeed a great Portion which has been given unto Me for thee ---

And I shall use discrimination and wisdom - for it is a foolish part to give unto fools that which has been guarded for eons by the wise ---

And I say unto thee: If ye are so minded and are prepared that ye may partake of this storehouse of wisdom -- And it shall be given unto thee to be brot within the great treasure vaults of Earth wherein are wonders most precious to behold! ---

I have prepared Myself for this age - and I am glad it is come for there shall be much Light released from the Higher realms -- And it shall be given unto man to know his Father and the fortune He has endowed him -- So be it that ye shall receive as ye are capable - and as ye ask - for it is the law that one <u>must</u> <u>ask</u> <u>and</u> <u>prepare</u> <u>himself</u>!

And as ye ask and apply thyself - many are sent that ye may be given in greater capacity -- So be it that ye shall enter the school of preparation - and ye shall be glad for thy preparation -- For it is now told thee that great changes shall come about of natural cause - and it shall behoove them to be prepared - for ye shall have a new place of abode ---

And it has been given unto many to say that - ye shall be prepared for a new place - and ye shall be given that which shall profit thee to accept in The Name of The Father - Son and Holy Ghost

I am thy Brother of The Emerald Cross - and in the Service of The Christ whom ye shall come to know -- So be it and Selah - Coro --

Blest of My Being: Ye have heard that which has been said unto thee - and now ye shall receive that which shall be given unto thee by the One which shall be sent unto Us from the place wherein the Beloved Marshea is -- And He shall give unto thee that which ye shall give unto them which await His Words ---

So be it that they shall be blest of Him - and that which He has for them -- So be it given unto thee in The Name of The Father - Son and Holy Ghost - Amen and Beleis ---

Romano

Blest of My Presence - and that which is given unto Me of the Most Worthy Grand Master: For I am come unto thee that ye shall have that which He has prepared for Me to bring unto thee -- And ye shall be prepared as a people to enter into the place which is prepared for thee ---

And in the time which is near I shall walk among thee - and I shall seek out them which are prepared to enter into My place of abode - and into the Temple of Osiris - for it is given unto many to be brot out of the Earth and into the place wherein I am -- For this

132

have I waited - for I am prepared to bring unto thee a Portion which shall awaken thee unto the vastness of the plan which has been prepared within the Inner Temple! ---

And ye shall be prepared to receive the "Greater Part" which has been kept for thee -- It is now time that ye be told that ye have been beguiled by the black dragon - which has created the veil of maya - and which has given thee the sleeping portion which ye shall have removed - and which shall be as a part of thy inheritance of the flesh and of the Earth ---

It shall be given unto thee to part the veil - and to have the stigma of darkness removed -- So shall ye know The Father and that which He has endowed thee -- And I stand ready to be thy hands and thy feet - as thou art prepared to receive of the new seed which We of the Higher realms proffer unto thee -- And ye shall be as the ones which shall profit by the presence of Them which are being sent to sibor thee -- And ye shall walk with Us and talk with Us - as ye give Us credence and port ---

As ye will it - so be it! For it is the better part of wisdom that ye seek Us out - for We are prepared to deliver thee out of darkness and that which shall be unto thee much torment---

I am given to patience and I shall await thy call - and I shall give unto thee as ye would have it -- For in no wise do We intrude on thy free will! So be ye of a mind to receive that which shall profit thee -- I am thy Brother and Sibor from the Temple of Osiris - and as The Father has sent Me unto thee - and in the Light of the Christ - I say - be ye about The Father's business which shall be unto thee thy

133

salvation -- And ye shall have more from this Source as ye are prepared to receive -- So be it and Selah –

I am Romano - of The Inner Temple of Osiris - and wherein ye which are prepared may be received in Love and Mercy - in The Name of The Most High ---

Sananda

Beloved who are My sheep - and who are as the ones which are waking and are beginning to stir: So be it that I have prepared a part for thee - and it shall contain within it that which shall profit thee if ye but see it - and if ye but ask for comprehension which shall be given thee ---

I am within My secret place of abode - and ye shall be given the particulars of that place and the work which goes on therein if ye but follow within My footsteps - for I am come into the Earth at this time that ye shall be enlightened on these things which is thy inheritance ---

And ye have but to seek Me out - and pray for discernment and I shall reveal Myself unto thee -- And I shall sibor thee in the way of the wise -- Yet it is given unto me to seek thee out - it is the <u>law that ye seek to find Me</u> -- For that have I waited - that ye may seek Me of thy own accord - and so shall it profit thee much ---

And I am in the place wherein I am prepared to receive them which are prepared to be brot into this place - for none shall pass into the Inner court unprepared -- It is given unto many to come into the Earth at this time that ye may be prepared for a new place of abode -- And it is My part to prepare the way for them that they may come into thy world - and to prepare the way that ye may enter into theirs ---

So be it that the great barrier shall be broken - and ye shall pass into other worlds - other planets - and ye shall be prepared even as We thy Sibors have been prepared for the parts We now have -- And it shall behoove every man to begin his search for the <u>open door</u> which has been opened thru the Grace and Mercy of The Most Worthy Grand Master of the Inner Temple -- So be it that all men shall be given his choice and as he prepares himself for his particular place - so it is prepared for him -- And as it is given unto every man to have free will it shall stand him four square to use it for his own betterment and for his own salvation ---

So be it as ye will it - for I can do no more than point the way - and bring ye to the gate -- And ye have but to enter and walk therein - for I am the Light and the Way -- Ye have forgotten thy covenant with Me which ye made in the beginning of thy sojourn within the Earth -- And so be it that ye shall remember and return unto thy Source -- And ye shall be in the place wherein ye are prepared to receive Me -- As ye calleth I shall answer thee in the Name of Our Father - Which has sent Me unto thee - and so be it and Beleis ---

I am thy Elder Brother - Sananda - of The Emerald Cross ---

Recorded by Sister Thedra of The Emerald Cross --

Part #25

Blest of my Being: Ye shall now receive of the one and only Posied - for He has prepared a part for thee - and ye shall give it unto them which are of a mind to receive of Him - and that which He has prepared for them -- So be it given in the Name of The Father Son and Holy Ghost -- Amen and Beleis ---

The Posied

Blest of My Being: Be ye as My hands present unto them which shall receive of My Words -- And within the time which is near ye shall be brot into the place wherein I am -- I have prepared a place for thee wherein ye may receive the <u>greater</u> <u>part</u> - which ye shall receive - for it is given unto Me to give the greater part and such is thy Inheritance -- So be it that ye have kept thy covenant with The Father - and He has kept thee for this day -- And now it is come that One shall come unto thee and He shall bring thee into the place wherein I am - And so be it that ye shall await His coming - and be ye blest of My Presence and that which I bring unto thee -- So be it that ye shall give unto them this part for they too shall be prepared for the greater part - and I am ready to give unto them as they are prepared to receive -- So be it that they shall receive as following:

Be ye blest of My Presence - and that which I am going to say unto thee - for it is My part to prepare thee as <u>a</u> <u>people</u> for a new place and a new part -- And as yet ye have not heard one word which has been said by the ones who have cried from the high places -- Lo the many times it has been said: "Prepare thyself! Prepare thyself!"

Now it is given unto Me to awaken thee - and many are sent unto the Earth for to alert thee ---

Ye look and see not! Ye have thy fingers in the ears - and ye hear not! As ye are aroused from thy sleep ye turn in thy bed and continue thy dreams - so be it that ye shall awaken! And so be it that it may be a rude awaking - for now it is come that there is no time for sleep - nor no place wherein ye may find to sleep --

I have given unto The Father My Word that ye shall be brot out of darkness - and I shall be true unto My Word - for I am prepared to keep it -- So be it that ye shall hear the Voice which calls from every part of the world - and it now echoes back thru the Cosmos -- So be ye quickened unto it - and bestir thyself - and many shall reach unto thee a hand which shall sustain thee and be unto thee strength and wisdom - for it is now come that ye shall be <u>sobered</u> -- And ye shall walk with equilibrium - and in the Light of the Christ -- For great Light shall be released from the Higher realms - and they which are not prepared to receive of it shall faint and fall -- And be it such as shall profit thee to reach out unto Them which would be unto thee thy deliverance out of darkness and torment ---

Blest are they which seek the Light for they shall find their way and therein is wisdom---

So be it that ye be blest of them which are sent into the Earth that ye may be delivered up -- And be it so - and so be it and Selah ---

I am thy Older Brother - The Posied - Of The Emerald Cross and the Temple of Osiris -- So shall ye come to know Me - for I am

137

within the Earth for that purpose - and be ye blest of The Most High - which ye shall come to know -- Selah --- will now give unto thee that which shall be given unto them -- For He has given unto thee that they may receive it - so be it and Beleis ---

Maroni (01)

Blest of My Being: Ye shall be blest for receiving Me - and being My hands made manifest unto them which have not prepared themself to receive of The Father - Son and Holy Ghost of their own account - for I am in the Inner Temple and I am prepared to prepare all which present themself for preparation -- So be it that ye shell give it unto them as I give it unto thee -- And it shall be given in The Name of The Father - Son and Holy Ghost which has given Me passport unto thee - and this is My Portion unto them:

Blest of my Being: I am 01 and known within thy records as Maroni - and for that matter I am little known in the Earth today for I have not spoken for a time -- And it is the way of man to forget that which has been said -- For they wish to sleep a while longer -- Yet I - as many of My Brothers and Sisters of the Inner Temple - am coming into the Earth that their sleep may be ended -- For it is now time to be awake and to know what is going on within the Higher realms -- Many have come unto thee that they may be aroused from their sleep - and that they may know which is given unto them of the Father - and all the Brothers of other realms Who so diligently are working to deliver them from their bondage ---

And it is given unto Me to come unto thee at this time to add My part to theirs -- For the veil is parted and the great void has been bridged -- Ye shall receive many from the place wherein I am --

And for the foregone years of silence wherein We did not come into the realm of men of Earth there has been much darkness - and for that matter there has been a great void between the realms of Light and the Earth -- And it shall be bridged by Light - The Light which never fails ---

So be ye of a mind to receive that which We of the Higher realms are prepared to bring unto thee ---

And now in this new dispensation We are permitted by the law of the Losolo to give unto thee in greater capacity - for We are not bound by this dispensation which has been fashioned in the Inner Temple -- And We have greater freedom from any part of the old law which was fashioned for them of another epoch - another age ---

Now it is given unto the children of Earth to fulfill that age - which is past! and to enter into a new age of Light -- And they shall know freedom from that which has bound them -- For their legirons shall be cut away - and they shall walk as they were meant to - as the Sons of God -- And they shall walk in the Light - and they shall become as Gods - which is the plan given unto Us of The Father - that they may become equal unto Him - for He has endowed them with all that He Is - and they have but to awaken unto their heritage -- And for that has the veil been rent -- And many shall step thru in Love and Wisdom - and so be it that I shall come unto thee and I shall sibor unto thee - and I shall sibor in ways which are beyond the comprehension of them which do not know Us ---

And We are the Guardians which shall be unto thee thy salvation in the time of stress -- So be it that all shall come to know Us and that which We have kept for this day -- So be it and Beleis --

I am come unto thee in The Name of The Father - Son and Holy Ghost - Amen and Beleis ---

I am thy Brother and Fellow of The Emerald Cross -- One which shall come again - and as ye ask of Me so shall I give unto thee - and Selah -- Maroni - of the place where all things are known ---

Beloved of My Being: I can give unto this Beloved Brother passport at any time - for He has given unto them of the Earth much - and they have forgotten so soon -- And now He has come unto thee many times - yet it was for thyself - and that which is for thee - keep for thyself - and that which is for them give unto them ---

So be it that He shall come into them which give Him port and credence - so be it that it shall profit them to receive of Him in The Name of The Father - Son and Holy Ghost - Amen and Beleis -- Sananda ---

Recorded by Sister Thedra of The Emerald Cross –

Made in the USA
Columbia, SC
14 February 2021